WALCH PUBLISHING

16 Extraordinary African Americans

Second Edition

Nancy Lobb

PHOTO CREDITS

SUSTAINABLE FORESTRY INITIATIVE

Certified Chain of Custody
Promoting Sustainable
Forest Management

www.sfiprogram.org

SGS-SFI/COC-US09/5501

1 2 3 4 5 6 7 8 9 10

ISBN 978-0-8251-6276-3

Copyright © 1995, 2007

J. Weston Walch, Publisher

P. O. Box 658 • Portland, Maine 04104-0658

www.walch.com

Printed in the United States of America

WALCH PUBLISHING®

Contents

To the Teacher

According to *Reading Next: A Vision for Action and Research in Middle and High School Literacy,* a report to the Carnegie Corporation of New York (2004, second edition), "High-interest, low-difficulty texts play a significant role in an adolescent literacy program and are critical for fostering the reading skills of struggling readers and the engagement of all students. In addition to using appropriate grade-level textbooks that may already be available in the classroom, it is crucial to have a range of texts in the classroom that link to multiple ability levels and connect to students' background experiences."

Biographies about extraordinary people are examples of one such kind of text. The 16 Americans described in this collection should both inspire and reassure students. As students read, your instruction can include approaches that will support not only comprehension, but also learning from passages.

Reading and language arts skills not only enrich students' academic lives but also their personal lives. The *Extraordinary Americans* series was written to help students gain confidence as readers. The biographies were written to pique students' interest while engaging their understanding of vocabulary, recalling facts, identifying the main idea, drawing conclusions, and applying knowledge. The added value of reading these biographies is that students will learn about other people and, perhaps, about themselves.

Students will read stories demonstrating that great things are accomplished by everyday people who may have grown up just like them—or maybe even with greater obstacles to overcome. Students will discover that being open to new ideas, working hard, and believing in one's self make them extraordinary people, too!

Structure of the Book

The Biographies

The collection of stories can be used in many different ways. You may assign passages for independent reading or engage students in choral reading. No matter which strategies you use, each passage contains pages to guide your instruction.

At the end of each passage, you will find a series of questions. The questions are categorized, and you can assign as many as you wish. The purposes of the questions vary:

- **Remembering the Facts:** Questions in this section engage students in a direct comprehension strategy, and require them to recall and find information while keeping track of their own understanding.

- **Understanding the Story:** Questions posed in this section require a higher level of thinking. Students are asked to draw conclusions and make inferences.

- **Getting the Main Idea:** Once again, students are able to stretch their thinking. Questions in this section are fodder for dialog and discussion around the extraordinary individuals and an important point in their lives.

- **Applying What You've Learned:** Proficient readers internalize and use the knowledge that they gain after reading. The question or activity posed allows for students to connect what they have read to their own lives.

In the latter part of the book, there are additional resources to support your instruction.

Vocabulary

A list of key words is included for each biography. The lists can be used in many ways. Assign words for students to define, use them for spelling lessons, and so forth.

Answer Key

An answer key is provided. Responses will likely vary for Getting the Main Idea and Applying What You've Learned questions.

Additional Activities

Extend and enhance students' learning! These suggestions include conducting research, creating visual art, exploring cross-curricular activities, and more.

References

Learn more about each extraordinary person or assign students to discover more on their own. Start with the sources provided.

To the Student

> "When the history books are written in future generations, the historians will have to pause and say, 'There lived a great people—a black people—who injected new meaning and dignity into the veins of civilization.'"
>
> —Dr. Martin Luther King Jr.

The lives of many African Americans have made a difference in the story of America. Writers, artists, scientists, teachers, politicians, ministers, lawyers, doctors, businesspeople, athletes, and so many more, have helped to make America what it is today. African Americans can be proud of their heritage. It is a pride all Americans should share.

In this book, you will read the stories of sixteen of these people:

- Sojourner Truth, a six-foot-tall traveling preacher whose powerful sermons showed many people that slavery was wrong

- Frederick Douglass, who called for an end to slavery

- Harriet Tubman, who led hundreds of slaves to freedom

- Ida B. Wells-Barnett, whose newspaper stories helped put an end to lynchings in the South

- Mary McLeod Bethune, who gave thousands of black children a chance for an education

- Booker T. Washington, who founded the Tuskegee Institute

- W.E.B. DuBois, who founded the NAACP and began the modern civil rights movement

- George Washington Carver, who found hundreds of uses for the peanut and turned agriculture around in the South

- Jackie Robinson, who broke the color barrier in professional baseball

- Thurgood Marshall, who became the first black Supreme Court justice

- Rosa Parks, whose simple actions began the civil rights movement

- Dr. Martin Luther King Jr., whose vision of nonviolence brought about giant strides for the civil rights movement

- Malcolm X, a militant who opposed Dr. King's views

- Jesse Jackson, who has become the leading black politician of our day

- Maya Angelou, poet laureate, who gives us an inspiring and optimistic view of our future

- Toni Morrison, an author who won the Nobel Prize for Literature

The motto on the Great Seal of the United States reads "E PLURIBUS UNUM." That is Latin for "Out of many, one." The United States is made up of many peoples of many races. These peoples have come together to form one nation. Each group has been an important part of American history. I hope you will enjoy reading about sixteen African Americans who have made a difference.

—Nancy Lobb

Sojourner Truth

Traveling Preacher

Seventy-year-old Sojourner Truth tried to board a Washington, DC, streetcar. But the conductor wouldn't stop for her. So when the next streetcar came along she stepped in front of it, yelling, "I want to ride!"

After boarding the car, she sat down in the white section. The conductor told her to move or get off. Truth refused. Finally, the car moved on. Truth had her ride.

After a number of other protests by Truth, the president of the streetcar company gave in. He told his conductors that they were to let everyone ride. And all riders could sit where they wished. Truth said, "The insides of the cars look like pepper and salt!"

This may sound like the civil rights movement of the 1950s and 1960s. But the story of Sojourner Truth took place over 100 years earlier. Her efforts laid the groundwork for the civil rights movement.

Sojourner Truth was born a slave in New York around 1797. Her real name was Isabella. But everyone called her Belle.

Belle was the ninth of ten children. All her brothers and sisters had already been sold as slaves. Belle's mother knew Belle could be sold at any time. So she taught Belle to ask God for help in times of trouble. Belle believed that God would always hear her and help.

Belle was nine years old when she was sold. She and her owners did not speak the same language. So Belle had a hard time following their directions. This led her owners to beat her.

Belle was sold three more times. Then, in 1810, she was sold to a farmer named John Dumont. She worked for him for 17 years. Dumont forced her to marry an older slave named Thomas. Together they had five children.

Belle's parents never got to see their grandchildren. Her mother died from an infection in her leg. Her father and two other old slaves were no longer able to work. They were sent away to live in a shack in the woods. Too weak to care for themselves, they died in the winter cold.

Finally a law was passed in New York. It said the slaves in that state would be freed on July 4, 1827. John Dumont told Belle that he would free her a year early if she worked hard. Belle worked hard. At the end of the year, he told her she hadn't worked hard enough.

Belle decided to run away. Taking only her youngest child, she left the others at Dumont's farm. She ran to the farm of a nearby Quaker family. The Quakers are a religious group who were against slavery. They were glad to help Belle.

Dumont followed Belle. He tried to take her back. The Quakers offered him $25 for Belle. He decided to take the money and go. The Quaker family freed Belle at once. At last she was a free woman!

Soon afterward, Dumont sold Belle's son Peter to a slave owner in Alabama. Peter was just five years old. Belle was upset. She knew that Peter would never be free in Alabama.

New York law said that no one could sell a slave to someone in another state. When Belle heard this, she took her case to court. It was one of the first times a black person had fought a white person in court.

Belle did not have a good chance of winning. She knew that being black and a woman worked against her. But she did win! The judge returned Peter to her.

Belle moved to New York City with Peter. She left her daughters with the Dumonts. But Peter never got over the abuse he had suffered in

Alabama. Peter got in trouble with the law. Finally, he ran off and became a sailor. Two years later he was lost at sea. Belle was heartsick.

In 1843, Belle decided to leave New York City. She felt God was telling her to leave her old life behind. Belle was 46 years old. Her daughters were grown. Her son and husband were dead. Belle was ready to move on.

Belle wanted a new name, too. She prayed about it. "The Lord gave me the name *Sojourner* because I was to travel up and down the land, showing people their sins, and being a sign unto them," she said. She gave herself the last name *Truth.* Thus Sojourner Truth started her new life.

In the 1840s, slaves in the United States had no rights. Women had no rights either. Many people began speaking out in favor of women's rights and against slavery. Sojourner Truth dedicated her life to these two causes.

Truth traveled from state to state. Everywhere she went, she spread her message. She was a powerful figure, six feet tall and extremely strong. Her singing and her preaching were powerful, too. She became famous. People flocked to hear her.

Sojourner Truth could not read or write. But in 1850 she had her life story published. It was called *The Narrative of Sojourner Truth: A Northern Slave.* By selling copies of the book, Truth made enough money to support herself.

After the Civil War ended in 1865, all slaves were free. But Truth knew her work was not over. Many former slaves had fled north and were living in camps called freedman's villages. Conditions in these camps were terrible!

Truth was nearly 70 years old, but she kept on working. She was put in charge of the Freedman's Hospital in Washington, DC. She made sure blacks had good medical care.

Truth kept fighting for her people until she was in her 80s. Just before she died, she told her children, "I'm not going to die; I'm going home like a shooting star." Sojourner Truth died on November 26, 1883, at the age of 86.

Sojourner Truth did not live to see her work finished. But many of the things she fought for now exist. Laws have been passed that give women and blacks their rights. The life of Sojourner Truth was the foundation upon which the rights of African Americans and women today were built.

Her fight for freedom would echo in the civil rights era nearly a century later. Her refusal to give up her seat on the streetcar was repeated by Rosa Parks in 1955. In 2002, a statue in Truth's honor was erected in Northampton, Massachusetts. Sojourner Truth's story remains inspiring to us today.

Remembering the Facts

1. How did Belle's mother prepare her for being sold to another slave owner?

2. Why did Belle run away from the Dumonts?

3. Why did the Quaker family help Belle?

4. Belle sued to get her son Peter back from Alabama. Why was this case so important?

5. Where did Belle get the name Sojourner Truth?

6. What two groups of people did Truth fight for?

7. What work did Truth do after the Civil War?

Understanding the Story

8. Why do you think so many antislavery activists also worked for women's rights?

9.   Why do you think so many people flocked to hear Sojourner Truth sing and preach?

10.   Why do you think her words had such an impact?

11.   Why do you think Sojourner Truth still felt she had work to do after slavery ended?

Getting the Main Idea

Why do you think Sojourner Truth was an important part of American history?

Applying What You've Learned

On October 29, 1864, Sojourner Truth met with President Abraham Lincoln. What do you think they might have talked about?

Frederick Douglass

Abolitionist Leader

Frederick Douglass was born a slave on a plantation in Maryland. His birth name was Frederick Bailey. Frederick never knew his mother. When he was a week old, she was sent to work 12 miles away.

It was the custom to take slave children away from their mothers at a very early age. Women who were too old to work in the fields cared for the children of the younger women. Frederick was raised by his grandmother.

When Frederick was six, his grandmother took him to the main plantation several miles away. She left him there to work. Frederick's older brother and two older sisters were working there, too. He had never seen them before.

The slave children were treated poorly. Their only food was cornmeal mush. This was placed in a trough. All the children had to eat at the same time. Some used their hands to eat. Some scooped the mush with oyster shells or bits of wood. The children fought over every bite of food. There was never enough.

But even worse than the hunger was the cold. The slave children wore only shirts that hung to their knees. No shoes. No pants. No blankets at night. On cold nights Frederick would steal an empty corn sack and crawl into it.

Even so, Frederick was better off than most slave children. He was chosen to be the companion of the plantation owner's young son, Daniel. Frederick ran errands and did whatever Daniel wanted.

When Frederick was seven or eight, he was sent to Baltimore. His job was to take care of the young son of Sophia and Hugh Auld. Frederick was thrilled to escape the plantation.

At first everything went well. Frederick liked his work. Sophia Auld was a kind woman who had never owned a slave before. So she treated him as she would treat any child. She even began teaching him to read.

When Hugh Auld found out that Frederick could read, he was furious! "If a slave learns to read, he'll be unfit to be a slave. A slave should know nothing but to obey his master," he said.

These words sank deep into Frederick's heart. At that moment he understood the path out of slavery to freedom. From then on, he had a fierce desire to read and learn.

But he would get no more help from Sophia. She would no longer allow him to read. And she no longer treated him well. The change in Sophia bothered Frederick. He saw that slavery was a "fatal poison" for the slave owner, too.

Frederick did learn to read and write. There were many poor white children in his neighborhood. When Frederick went out, he carried extra bread with him. He traded this bread for reading lessons from the white children.

When Frederick was 15, he was sent back to the plantation. His owners soon found that he would not obey his master.

Finally, he was sent to a slave-breaker. The slave-breaker was a man who treated slaves badly to "break" them. The purpose was to teach them to obey their masters.

For almost a year Frederick was forced to work long hours with little food. He was whipped every day. One day he fought back. He stopped the slave-breaker from beating him.

The slave-breaker knew then he would never break Frederick. But he didn't want anyone else to find out. He sent Frederick back to Baltimore to Hugh and Sophia Auld.

It was 1838. Frederick was 18 years old. Every day he dreamed of freedom. Frederick borrowed some sailor clothes and some money. He bought a train ticket to Philadelphia. He borrowed papers from a friend showing that he was a free black.

If anyone checked the papers closely, they would find out he was a runaway slave. But no one did. Frederick made it to freedom. He changed his name to Frederick Douglass so slave catchers would not find him. And he sent for, and married, his sweetheart, Anna.

Douglass had been free only a few months when he got involved in the abolitionist movement. He began traveling throughout the northern states giving speeches against slavery.

In May 1845, he published his life story, titled *Narrative of the Life of Frederick Douglass, an American Slave.*

In his book, Douglass showed the cruelty of slavery. He showed how slavery destroys the spirit of both slave and owner. The book made Douglass famous.

Now Douglass's owner now knew where he was and came after him. Douglass fled to England for safety. He spent two years there lecturing on slavery. Finally, two English friends sent money to Hugh Auld and bought Douglass's freedom. Douglass returned to America.

Douglass was free. But many others were not. He began working for the freedom of all slaves in America.

Douglass was now the most famous black leader in America. He was in demand as a speaker and a writer. Douglass moved his family to Rochester, New York. There he began a newspaper. He named it *The North Star,* because runaway slaves followed the North Star to freedom.

In 1861, the Civil War began. Then, in 1863, President Abraham Lincoln freed the slaves. Douglass met with Lincoln in the White House. He asked that blacks be allowed to join the Union Army.

Douglass's two sons joined the army. But they were not treated fairly. Black solders were paid half of what white soldiers were paid. Blacks got poor training and weapons.

Douglass told Lincoln that black and white soldiers die the same. They should be paid the same. Lincoln made sure that they were.

After the war was over, Douglass continued to work for the rights of the freed slaves. President Rutherford B. Hayes made Douglass U.S. Marshal of the District of Columbia in 1877.

In 1880, President James Garfield asked Douglass to be recorder of deeds for Washington, DC. In 1881, Douglass published his autobiography, *Life and Times of Frederick Douglass.*

Douglass was appointed U.S. ambassador to Haiti in 1889. Haiti was the world's oldest black republic. So Douglass was pleased with the job. Two years later, he resigned due to ill health.

Douglass spoke out all his life for black rights and women's rights. His ideas would strongly influence those who followed him: W.E.B. DuBois, Booker T. Washington, and Ida Wells-Barnett, among others.

On February 20, 1895, Douglass died. No one had struggled harder for the rights of his people. Frederick Douglass had been a powerful voice for freedom.

Remembering the Facts

1. Why did Douglass first meet his brother and sisters when he was six years old?

2. How were the slave children treated badly?

3. Why was Hugh Auld angry when he found out his wife had taught Douglass to read?

4. Why was Douglass sent to a slave-breaker?

5. How did Douglass escape from slavery?

6. Why did Douglass name his newspaper *The North Star*?

7. Name one job Douglass held after the Civil War.

Understanding the Story

8. Why do you think slave children were often separated from their mothers at an early age?

9.   Why do you think it was against the law to teach slaves to read?

10.   Why do you think Douglass said that slavery poisoned both slave and owner?

Getting the Main Idea

Why do you think Frederick Douglass is an important part of American history?

Applying What You've Learned

Imagine yourself as a slave (your age) living in the early 1800s. Describe a typical day in your life.

Harriet Tubman

The African-American Moses

Harriet Tubman was born into slavery. But even as a child she dreamed of freedom. Not until she was 29 did she escape to the free state of Pennsylvania.

Later, she told how she felt when she knew she was free. "I looked at my hands to see if I was the same person now that I was free. There was such a glory over everything. The sun came like gold through the trees, and over the fields. I felt like I was in heaven."

Living in Philadelphia, Tubman learned about the Underground Railroad. This was a secret network of people who helped runaway slaves.

Several routes were set up from the South to the North. "Railroad stations" were really homes of people who sheltered the slaves along the route. "Conductors" were those who led the slaves along the route.

Tubman became a conductor on the Underground Railroad. She led more slaves to freedom than anyone else. Alone, she made 19 trips back to the South. She led 300 slaves to freedom. Tubman said, "On my Underground Railroad, I never ran my train off the track. And I never lost a passenger."

Harriet Tubman was born in 1822 on a plantation near Cambridge, Maryland. She was one of nine children. Harriet and her family were all slaves. But their family was a loving one. Harriet's parents gave her a strong faith and love for her fellow humans.

When she was six years old, Harriet's master began renting her out to nearby families to do housework. Harriet worked hard. But she was not happy.

Her owner sent her to work in the fields. This was usually a man's job, and Harriet was only seven years old. She learned to plow, chop wood, and hoe weeds.

One day, when Harriet was eleven, she saw a slave trying to escape. The slave ran, with the overseer chasing him. The overseer threw a heavy lead weight at the man. Harriet tried to shield him. The weight hit her in the forehead.

Harriet was in a coma for weeks. As she slept, she had the same dream over and over. Beautiful women called out to her, "Come. Arise. Flee for your life."

Finally, she woke up. It was months before she could walk. For the rest of her life, she had seizures. Several times a day—without warning—she would drop and fall into a deep sleep.

When she was 22, Harriet was allowed to marry a free black man, John Tubman. But Harriet never forgot her dream of freedom. She told herself, "I must take my freedom, because surely no one is going to give it to me!"

In 1849, Harriet Tubman learned that her master planned to sell her to someone in the South. So Tubman ran away. She hid all day. At night she followed the North Star. Weeks later, she made it to freedom!

But Tubman didn't forget her family or her people. After working for a year to save money, she began making return trips to the South to free others. By 1857, she had freed her entire family—including her parents, who were then in their 70s. She made her last trip south in 1861.

In these years, Tubman also worked with the abolitionist movement (the movement to free the slaves) in the North. She gave speeches for black rights and women's rights. White abolitionist leaders gave Tubman money for her work.

During the Civil War, Tubman worked as a nurse for the Union Army. She set up slave spy networks deep in the South. She also acted as an army scout.

Tubman even led a series of raids against the South. On one of these raids, 800 slaves were rescued. Tubman became the first woman to lead U.S. Army troops in battle!

After the Civil War, Tubman raised money to support schools for former slaves. She collected clothing for the poor. And she worked to establish homes for the elderly. In 1908, she opened a home for elderly and needy blacks: The Harriet Tubman Home for Aged and Indigent Colored People.

Harriet Tubman's story is one of strength and courage. She acted as she did out of a sense of duty and justice. Never did she work for wealth or fame. Tubman died penniless on March 10, 1913.

But this tiny woman, under five feet tall, was a giant of a heroine. Frederick Douglass once said to her, "The midnight sky and the silent stars have been the witnesses of your devotion to freedom and of your heroic acts." Harriet Tubman is remembered today as one of America's greatest heroes.

Remembering the Facts

1. What kind of work did Tubman do at age seven?

2. Why did Harriet have seizures?

3. Why did Harriet Tubman decide to escape in 1849?

4. How many trips south did Tubman make to rescue slaves?

5. What was the abolitionist movement?

6. What was one way Tubman helped the Union Army?

7. List something Tubman did after the Civil War ended.

Understanding the Story

8. Why do you think Harriet Tubman became a popular folk heroine?

9. Why do you think Tubman returned to the South again and again after escaping to freedom?

10. Why do you think Tubman worked for women's rights?

Getting the Main Idea

Why do you think Harriet Tubman is an important part of American history?

Applying What You've Learned

Imagine you are a slave trying to escape to freedom. Write a paragraph telling about a day on the run. What happens to you? What are you feeling and thinking?

Ida B. Wells-Barnett

Newspaperwoman

Ida B. Wells was born a slave in Holly Springs, Mississippi, in 1862. She was a baby when Abraham Lincoln freed the slaves. Her parents were joyful! They hoped their little girl would have an easier life than they had had.

Wells was the oldest of eight children. Her father worked as a carpenter. The family had little money, but they remained strong. Her parents stressed the importance of hard work and education.

Wells attended Rust College in Holly Springs. She was an excellent student. She liked to read. But she especially loved to write.

Ida Wells had a happy childhood. But all that changed suddenly in the summer of 1878. An outbreak of yellow fever claimed the lives of her parents and youngest brother. At the age of 16, Wells was left to care for her younger brothers and sisters.

For a year, Wells kept her family together. She taught school, earning $25 a month. The next year she took a higher-paying job near Memphis. Other family members took care of the younger children.

Wells' lifelong fight against injustice toward blacks began on a train ride to work one day. She bought a first-class ticket. Then she sat down in the first-class section as she always did. The conductor came by to collect tickets. He told her she would have to move to the black car. Wells refused and was forced off the train.

Ida Wells sued the railroad. She won the case and was awarded $500! But her success did not last. The railroad appealed the case. The higher court overturned the verdict. She had to pay back the $500, plus court costs.

The Living Way, a black church newspaper, asked her to write a story about her fight with the railroad. The editor liked her writing so much he asked Wells to do a weekly column.

Editors of other black papers began using Ida's work. Soon she was writing for major black newspapers all over the country. She continued to teach school as well.

After the Civil War, the black press took on an important role in the South. From 1866 on, black newspapers were published in nearly every state. Their goal was to help educate the newly freed blacks.

In 1889, Wells became editor and part owner of *The Memphis Free Speech*. She was well known for her militant views. After writing about the poor quality of education for blacks in the Memphis schools, she was fired from her teaching job.

The next year, three black men opened a grocery store in Memphis. It was across the street from a white store. The owners of the white store became angry when they lost business to the black store. The black owners were kidnapped and lynched.

African Americans were furious. *The Memphis Free Speech* encouraged them to leave Memphis and move west. Thousands did just that.

Ida Wells went on the attack. She wrote about the lynchings and beatings of blacks. She spoke out against unfair treatment of blacks.

Wells left town on a business trip. While she was gone, a group of whites burned the office of the newspaper. She was warned never to come back to Memphis. If she did, she was told, she would be hanged in front of the courthouse.

Wells moved to New York City. She was offered a job at *The New York Age.* Here she kept on with her war on lynchings.

Between 1887 and 1896, over 1,000 blacks were lynched in the South. Wells traveled throughout the northern United States and England, speaking against lynching.

Wells wrote several books. *Southern Horrors: Lynch Law in All Its Phases* was written in 1892. In 1895, she wrote *The Red Record.* It showed that thousands of black men, women, and children had been lynched.

In 1895, she met Ferdinand Barnett, a lawyer and a newspaper owner. They were married and had four children.

Wells-Barnett continued to speak all over the country. She met with President McKinley. He supported her in her fight against lynching.

Many people were shocked at the violence going on in the South. They formed clubs called Ida B. Wells Clubs. Their slogan was "No More Lynching!"

In 1908, there was a race riot in Springfield, Illinois. Many blacks were killed. Black leaders met in New York City to take action. Out of this meeting came the NAACP (National Association for the Advancement of Colored People). Wells-Barnett was one of the group's founders.

Wells-Barnett also founded the Negro Fellowship League in Chicago. This group provided low-cost housing and an employment center for homeless men.

Ida B. Wells-Barnett died in 1931 at the age of 69. After her death, the Chicago Housing Authority opened the Ida B. Wells Housing Project in her memory.

Remembering the Facts

1. Why was Ida B. Wells thrown off the train on a trip to Memphis?

2. What was the final outcome of her suit against the railroad?

3. How did Wells get started on her writing career?

4. What was the subject of most of her writing?

5. What was the slogan of the Ida B. Wells Clubs?

6. What national group did Ida B. Wells-Barnett co-found?

7. What was the purpose of the Negro Fellowship League?

8. How did the Chicago Housing Authority honor Wells-Barnett?

Understanding the Story

9. Why do you think black newspapers were so important to the black community after the Civil War?

10. Ida B. Wells-Barnett worked all her life to stop violence in America. If she were writing newspaper articles today, what issues do you think she would write about?

Getting the Main Idea

Why do you think Ida B. Wells-Barnett is an important part of American history?

Applying What You've Learned

Imagine that you are Ida B. Wells-Barnett. Write a newspaper article about a problem related to violence in your community. Give your ideas for solving that problem.

Mary McLeod Bethune

Teacher with a Dream

Mary McLeod Bethune's dream was to make education available to every African American. She believed that education was the only way blacks could escape their lives of hard work and poverty.

In the early 1900s, there were few schools for blacks. Bethune devoted her life to changing that fact.

Mary McLeod was born in Mayesville, South Carolina, in 1875. She was the fifteenth of seventeen children. Her parents and her fourteen older siblings were former slaves.

Mary's parents were hard workers. They saved their money until they were able to buy a small farm. As a young girl, Mary worked a full day picking cotton. At night she did household chores.

After dinner, the family read from the Bible and sang hymns. Mary's parents taught her that those who have a strong faith and who work hard serving others are rewarded. These ideas would stay with her all her life.

No one in Mary's family had ever been to school. In 1882, a church mission school for black children was founded in Mayesville. Mary's parents allowed her to go because she had such a strong desire to learn to read. So she walked the five miles to school each day.

Mary used her reading and math skills to help poor whites and blacks. She made sure farmers were paid fairly for their cotton. She checked the amounts they were billed at the village store.

After four years at the mission school, she won a scholarship to Scotia Seminary for black women in Concord, North Carolina. The entire village was excited!

Mary's parents had no money for her clothes and school supplies. So everyone pitched in. One person gave her stockings. Another made over a dress to fit her.

On the day she left, the entire village stopped work. They walked for miles to the train station to see off twelve-year-old Mary McLeod. No one had ever even heard of anyone going away to school!

Mary studied at Scotia for six years. Then she entered Moody Bible Institute in Chicago. She hoped to become a missionary to Africa. But she was in for a big disappointment. The Mission Board told her that they only sent white missionaries to Africa!

Mary found her mission teaching the African-American children of her own country. She returned to the South. She spent five years teaching in Georgia and South Carolina.

In South Carolina, she met Albertus Bethune. They married and had one son, Albert Bethune. Theirs was not a happy marriage. Albertus thought Mary spent too much time on her work. Eight years later, they parted.

In 1900, Mary was teaching at a mission school in Palatka, Florida. She read about the thousands of black workers going to Daytona Beach, Florida, to work on the East Coast Railroad. She knew there were no schools for the children of these workers. This was a great chance to start her own school!

In 1904, Mary founded the Daytona Educational and Industrial Institute. Her assets were "five little girls, a dollar and a half, and faith in God." Her students were taught both academics and work skills such as broom-making.

Mary was determined and full of energy. To raise money for her school, she baked pies and sold them to the railroad workers. She and her students put on musical performances. Her students worked in the community doing chores. Mary dug through the town dump looking for furniture, dishes, and lumber. The school grew. In two years, she had 250 students.

Mary never missed a chance to tell people about her school. She also worked hard to improve life for the entire black community. She was a tireless fundraiser. She would ask her listeners to "invest in a human soul."

Mary won the support of Daytona's black and white leaders. She got funds from wealthy white winter residents. By 1922, she had a thriving school with a staff of twenty-five.

In 1929, the school merged with the Cookman Institute. It was then known as Bethune-Cookman College. Mary was president of the college until 1942.

Mary began other work when she was over 60 years old. She headed the National Association of Colored Women. She was also president of the National Council of Negro Women.

Mary was also the first black woman to head a federal agency. In 1936, she was named director of the Division of Negro Affairs in the National Youth Administration. This agency was created by Franklin D. Roosevelt to fight unemployment among youth.

Mary started a group called the Black Cabinet. This group advised Roosevelt on issues affecting blacks. She was able to channel large amounts of money into education and job training for blacks.

Mary McLeod Bethune was 79 when she died. When she knew she was dying, Mary wrote a letter to all African Americans. In it she shared the ideals she lived by.

Here, then, is my legacy:

I leave you love.
I leave you hope.
I leave you a thirst for education.
I leave you faith.
I leave you dignity.
I leave you a desire to live in harmony
with your fellow man.

—Mary McLeod Bethune

Remembering the Facts

1. What did Bethune think was the way out of poverty?

2. Why was Bethune unable to be a missionary to Africa?

3. Why did Bethune choose Daytona Beach as the location for her new school?

4. What were three ways Bethune and her students raised money for the school?

5. What college was Bethune president of for 13 years?

6. What was the purpose of the Black Cabinet?

7. What were three things Bethune left to African Americans in her legacy?

Understanding the Story

8. Bethune often said she had a rich life, even though she was born and died poor. In what ways do you think her life was rich?

9. Bethune once said, "Without faith, nothing is possible. With it, nothing is impossible." How do you think she lived these words in her own life?

10. Martin Luther King Jr. said, "If you want to be important, wonderful. If you want to be great, wonderful. But recognize that he who is greatest among you shall be your servant." King knew that true greatness comes through service to others. How did Bethune show this in her life?

Getting the Main Idea

Why do you think Mary McLeod Bethune is an important part of American history?

Applying What You've Learned

How can you apply the message in Bethune's legacy to your own life?

Booker T. Washington

Founder of the Tuskegee Institute

It was 1895. In Atlanta, Georgia, the Cotton States Exposition was being held. The plan was to get northern whites to invest in cotton. Booker T. Washington had been asked to talk about the black workers.

Washington rose to speak to the crowd. Many people were shocked! They couldn't believe a black man had been asked to speak.

Washington began by saying that blacks and whites in the South should get along. He said that blacks should become educated. But until they did, they should be content being "on the bottom of life, not the top." The races could stay as separate as the fingers on the hand. Yet, like the fingers on a hand, they could work together for a common goal.

Washington went on. He said blacks should put off their demands for civil rights. They should be patient. Civil rights would come one day when they had earned them.

The white audience leaped to its feet and cheered. The speech was repeated across the country. It became known as the Atlanta Compromise. In an instant, Booker T. Washington had become the most famous black of his time.

Booker T. Washington was born a slave on a Virginia farm in 1856. After the Civil War, his family moved to West Virginia. Washington, his brother, and his father worked in the salt mines. It was hard work—from dawn to dusk—for little pay.

Washington wanted to better himself. In the salt mines, he taught himself to read the numbers on the salt barrels. One evening, his mother gave him a *Webster's Speller*. From this he taught himself the alphabet and simple words.

One day, a school for blacks was formed nearby. Washington began attending night school. Then he heard about the Hampton Institute, an industrial school for blacks in Virginia.

At age 16, he walked the 200 miles to the school. He arrived there dirty and without a penny. He worked his way through Hampton as a janitor. When he graduated, he became a teacher in his old hometown. Four years later, he returned to teach at Hampton. In 1881, Washington left Hampton for Tuskegee, Alabama. There he founded the Tuskegee Institute, a school for black students.

Building the school was an uphill struggle. The Alabama legislature would pay the teachers. But there was no money for land, buildings, or equipment.

Washington found a site for the school south of town. It was a hilly 100-acre spread with several shacks on it. Working tirelessly, he was able to get $500 in donations to buy the land.

The school opened with 30 students. Over the next ten years, Washington built the school into the largest black school in the United States. Wealthy whites such as John D. Rockefeller and Andrew Carnegie gave large sums of money to the school.

Tuskegee offered basic elementary school subjects. But its real focus was teaching trades such as carpentry and brick-making. Washington felt that by learning a trade, blacks could become useful to white society. He said, "The person who can do something the world wants will make his way regardless of his race."

It is easy to see why whites liked his views. Washington was not a threat to them. Before long, he had won friends across the country. He became an advisor to Presidents Theodore Roosevelt and Grover Cleveland. Booker T. Washington had become the spokesperson for his race.

In 1901, Washington wrote the story of his life. It was called *Up From Slavery.* This book is still in print today!

But by the early 1900s, many blacks were tired of Washington's ideas for solving the race problem. Things weren't getting any better. Blacks were not allowed to vote. Segregation was getting worse. And blacks were being lynched in record numbers.

Many educated northern blacks, such as W.E.B. DuBois, felt Washington's ideas were blocking black progress. DuBois felt blacks should not be content to be second-class citizens. He thought they should demand their rights. The Washington-DuBois debate lasted for many years.

Booker T. Washington died on November 13, 1915. He was buried on the campus of his beloved Tuskegee Institute.

After Washington's death, W.E.B. DuBois said, "He was the greatest black leader since Frederick Douglass. On the other hand, in stern justice, we must lay upon the soul of this man a heavy responsibility for the loss of the Negro right to vote, the decline of the Negro college and public school, and the firmer establishment of the color caste."

This is the image of Washington that many people have today. However, it may be that he took the only course he could, living as he did in the deep South right after the Civil War. Even though many blacks later disliked his ideas, no one could argue with his real goal of justice and equality for all.

"We must learn to think not in terms of race or color or language or religion … but in terms of humanity," Washington once said. This message is still true today.

The legacy of Booker T. Washington lives on in the Tuskegee Institute. Today, it is known as Tuskegee University. The campus has 75 buildings. It offers more than 50 programs to its 3,000 students. A monument on the campus honors Washington for helping so many others see the value of education.

Remembering the Facts

1. What was the name given to the speech Washington gave at the Cotton States Exposition?

2. Why did Washington say blacks were not ready to have civil rights?

3. What school did Washington go to when he was 16?

4. What school did Washington found in Alabama?

5. How did Washington fund his school?

6. Why did some blacks disagree with Washington's ideas?

7. What two presidents did Washington advise?

Understanding the Story

8. Why do you think whites liked Booker T. Washington's ideas for solving race problems?

9. Why do you think Washington emphasized trades rather than
    academic subjects at Tuskegee?

10. How do you think some whites used Washington's story about
    fingers on the hand to justify segregation?

Getting the Main Idea

Why do you think Booker T. Washington is an important part of
American history?

Applying What You've Learned

After the Civil War, many former slaves did not know what to do with
their newfound freedom. Write a paragraph that tells about some of the
changes you think they would have had to deal with.

W.E.B. DuBois

Scholarly Leader

It was August 28, 1963. A quarter of a million Americans of all races had gathered in Washington, DC. They were there to take a stand against racial injustice. The huge crowd marched together to the Lincoln Memorial. Martin Luther King Jr. gave his famous speech in which he said, "I have a dream!" As the day went on, the word spread.

W.E.B. DuBois had died the night before. Most of the people did not know who he was. But those who knew were deeply moved by the news of his passing.

Roy Wilkins, leader of the NAACP (National Association for the Advancement of Colored People), explained to the crowd: "At the dawn of this century his was the voice that was calling to you to gather here today." DuBois had paved the road for those who were marching that day. His work was not understood by most Americans until years later.

William Edward Burghardt DuBois's early life was very different from that of most American blacks of his time. He was born in a small Massachusetts town in 1868. DuBois's parents were free blacks who had never been slaves.

DuBois's father left his family when DuBois was a year old. His mother, Mary, was left to raise him on her own. Mary knew that education was the key to success. So she worked hard to keep him in school.

There was little racism in DuBois's hometown. He went to school with white children. Because he was a gifted student, he was accepted by the best families in town.

DuBois graduated from high school with honors. The townspeople raised enough money to send him to Fisk University in Tennessee. DuBois wanted to go to Harvard, but it was too much money. It was Fisk or nothing. So, in 1885, he set off for Tennessee—south into "the land of the slaves."

DuBois took all the classes offered at Fisk. But he was learning other things, too. For the first time, he saw racial prejudice.

DuBois wrote, "I was tossed boldly into the Negro problem. I came to a place where the world was split into white and black halves. The darker half was held back by prejudice and by law, as well as by ignorance and poverty."

During the summer, DuBois taught in a country school. Here poor farmers sent their children. The school was a windowless hut with a dirt floor. There were few books. Finally, DuBois saw how most blacks lived.

DuBois decided to devote his life to making better lives for American blacks. To be a better leader, he got the best education he could.

DuBois got his wish. Harvard gave him a scholarship. He graduated with honors. Then he studied for two years at the University of Berlin in Germany.

In 1895, he received his Ph.D. from Harvard. This made him the first black to earn Harvard's highest degree. He said, "The years of study were over. Life was about to begin."

DuBois took a teaching job at the University of Pennsylvania. He began to write a book about blacks' daily life in the city. It was called *The Philadelphia Negro: A Social Study.*

DuBois moved on to Atlanta University in 1897. Here he continued to study the problems faced by black Americans.

DuBois became a black leader. He called for black rights. He spoke out against lynchings and segregation. He supported black art and literature. He asked for support of black businesses.

In 1903, DuBois wrote *The Souls of Black Folk*. It became his best-known writing.

In the book he said, "The problem of the twentieth century is the problem of the color line." He said the "talented tenth" of blacks must be leaders. By this he meant that educated blacks must lead the others to a better life.

DuBois's ideas caused a major debate among blacks. Booker T. Washington had said they should not worry about their rights. They should work to better themselves. Civil rights would come later when blacks were ready for them.

DuBois said Booker T. Washington was wrong! He thought blacks should have their rights at once. He believed that educated blacks should work with whites. Then both races would learn to respect each other.

DuBois's ideas launched the civil rights movement. He helped found the NAACP (National Association for the Advancement of Colored People) in 1910.

For 24 years, he edited *The Crisis*, the journal of the NAACP. The NAACP became the leading civil rights group in America.

DuBois also worked for racial equality around the world, especially in Africa. DuBois thought of Africa as the homeland of American blacks.

In fact, W.E.B. DuBois spent his last years in Ghana, West Africa. He moved there in 1961 to work on a study of African blacks. He continued to work for equality until his death in 1963 at the age of 95.

Remembering the Facts

1. How was DuBois' childhood different from that of most black Americans of his time?

2. What made DuBois aware of the problems faced by most blacks?

3. What was the theme of *The Souls of Black Folk?*

4. What group did DuBois help found in 1910?

5. Why did DuBois want to get a high level of education?

6. Where did DuBois spend the last years of his life?

7. What was DuBois' last project?

Understanding the Story

8. DuBois wrote, "The problem of the twentieth century is the problem of the color line." What do you think he meant? Do you agree? Explain your answer.

9. DuBois called for the "talented tenth" of blacks to lead. Do you think that educated blacks today have met this challenge? Explain your answer.

10. Booker T. Washington called on African Americans to accept where they were, work hard, and wait for things to get better one day. Why do you think DuBois disagreed with this idea?

Getting the Main Idea

Why do you think W.E.B. DuBois is an important part of American history?

Applying What You've Learned

DuBois called those who were successful in business or a profession the "talented tenth." He believed that the first duty of the upper class was to serve the lower classes. What do you think he meant? Do you agree?

George Washington Carver

Botanist

It was 1921. The United States House Ways and Means Committee was meeting. Committee members were debating about putting a tax on peanuts imported from other countries. Such a tax would help the peanut farmers of America.

George Washington Carver had come to speak to the committee about peanuts. He came into the room carrying an old suitcase. He was dressed in an old suit that looked as if it had been slept in. In his lapel he wore a flower. The chairman of the committee was not impressed. He gave Carver ten minutes to speak.

Carver began to talk. His voice was odd and high-pitched. He said he was an agricultural scientist at Tuskegee Institute in Alabama. "The peanut," he said, "is one of the most remarkable crops that we are all acquainted with." And from his suitcase, he began to bring out some of the 280 products he had made from peanuts.

By this time, his ten minutes were up. The chairman told Carver he could have ten more minutes. Carver was given more time again and again.

Finally, the chairman told Carver he could talk for as long as he wanted. And he did. One by one he told about each product he had made. He did so with wit and showmanship.

The committee was amazed. They passed the tax on imported peanuts. And they invited Carver to come back with more peanut products!

This story soon made its way into the newspapers. George Washington Carver became the first educated African-American to become a national folk hero.

George Washington Carver was born in Missouri in 1864. His mother was a slave on a farm owned by the Carvers. When George was a baby, he and his mother were kidnapped from the Carvers' farm by slave raiders. A neighbor went in search of them. He found baby George alone by the side of the road. His mother was never found.

Carver was a sickly baby. The kidnapping nearly killed him. His owners moved him and his brother into their own house and raised them.

Carver had many chores to do around the farm. But when the work was done, he was free to explore. He spent many hours collecting plants, animals, and rocks that interested him. Even as a small boy it was clear he had a "green thumb." He became known in the area as the "plant doctor." Neighbors asked him to help with their problem plants.

Carver's love of nature led him to become deeply religious. The wonders of nature showed him that God was everywhere. He believed that by learning more about God's creation he could learn more about God.

Carver had an overwhelming desire to learn. Mrs. Carver taught him to read. Then she got him a tutor. But soon Carver knew more than his teacher. At age twelve, he left home to attend a school for blacks. After about one year, he found he knew more than his teacher at school, too.

For the next ten years, Carver earned a living doing odd jobs. He picked up any education he could. He took up painting and found that he had a gift as an artist. Most of his paintings were of wildflowers and plants. In 1890, he went to Simpson College in Iowa to study art.

Carver knew that it would be hard for a black man to make a living as an artist. So he changed his field of study to botany, the study of plants. Carver went to Iowa State College. He was the outstanding agricultural student on campus. After he got his master's degree, he stayed on as a teacher.

Carver's work became known to scientists around the country. He began getting many job offers.

In 1896, Booker T. Washington asked Carver to teach at the Tuskegee Institute in Alabama. Carver accepted the offer. He wanted to use his knowledge to help poor southern blacks better themselves. He said, "To this end I have been preparing myself for these many years. This kind of education is the key to unlock the door of freedom to our people." Carver was to work at Tuskegee for the next 50 years.

Carver's skills were indeed needed. Farmland in much of America was getting worn out. Carver said that much of the soil in the South was "practically a pile of sand and clay."

Carver knew that farmers needed to rotate crops. He urged farmers to plant more than one crop. He said they should change where they planted each crop every year.

They also needed to fertilize the soil. This could be done with manure. They could start a compost heap. Farmers could also plow under the leftover stalks of plants that had already been harvested. These three ways of organic farming put nutrients back in the soil at no cost to the farmer.

Carver did experiments that showed how well crop rotation and soil building worked. For 40 years, his findings were printed in "Bulletins" that were given free to farmers.

Carver worked in his lab. He found many uses for the peanut and the sweet potato. This was the part of his work that made him famous. But his most important contribution was the help he gave to farmers.

All Carver's work was done with the small farmer in mind. His goal was to be "of the greatest good to the greatest number of my people." In 1897, Carver began holding monthly meetings for farmers at Tuskegee. In the winter of 1907, he taught a free Short Course in Agriculture. He also drove through the countryside to share materials and ideas with farmers.

By the 1920s, all of America had heard of "The Wizard of Tuskegee." Thomas Edison asked Carver to work for him and offered a huge salary. But Carver felt he should stay in the South, where he could be of greater service. He received many honors from black and white groups. But he was happiest working in his lab. He still wanted to help the "man farthest down."

On January 5, 1943, George Washington Carver died. He was buried at Tuskegee Institute. On his tombstone are these words:

> "He could have added fortune to fame, but caring for neither, he found happiness and honor in being helpful to the world."

Remembering the Facts

1. Which part of his work brought Carver national fame?

2. How did Carver show a talent for botany as a boy?

3. Why did Carver change his college major from art to botany?

4. Where did Carver work for over 50 years?

5. What is crop rotation?

6. Name two ways of organic farming taught by Carver.

7. Name two ways Carver gave information to small farmers.

Understanding the Story

8. George Washington Carver became a folk hero in his time.
    Thomas Edison offered him a huge salary to work for him. Why
    do you think Carver chose to stay in the rural South?

9. Carver was a close friend of both Thomas Edison and Henry Ford. How do you think these three men were alike?

10. Carver emphasized using organic farming methods. How do you think these views would fit in with today's science of ecology?

Getting the Main Idea

Why do you think George Washington Carver is an important part of American history?

Applying What You've Learned

George Washington Carver did many experiments involving crossbreeding. This happens when a new plant is made that combines the features of two kinds of plants. The new plant is called a *hybrid*.

Imagine you're a scientist. Develop a hybrid plant that combines two existing plants. Give your new plant a name. Draw it. Give a short description of it.

Jackie Robinson

Baseball Star

It was 1946. World War II had ended. Thousands of black soldiers had fought and died in the war. But there were still no blacks in professional baseball.

Branch Rickey was the president of the Brooklyn Dodgers. He decided it was time for a change. African Americans should be playing major league ball.

The first black player in pro baseball would have to be an outstanding player. But he would need to be mentally tough, too. He would have to be able to stand up to abuse without fighting back. He would have to face prejudice with courage.

For three years, Rickey and his scouts looked for the right man. Finally, Rickey found the man he wanted: Jackie Robinson.

Rickey met with Robinson. He told him how he must handle himself. He must not show anger. He must not strike out when yelled at or threatened.

Robinson listened, then asked, "Mr. Rickey, do you want a ballplayer who's afraid to fight back?"

Rickey answered, "I want a player with guts enough not to fight back." Jackie Robinson thought hard. Finally, he agreed. Jackie Robinson was a success. And his success opened up pro sports to other black athletes.

Jackie Robinson was born on January 31, 1919, in Cairo, Georgia. When Robinson was six months old, his father left the family.

Robinson's mother took her five children to live in Pasadena, California. She worked long hours doing housework for other families to support her children.

The family moved to a small house in a white neighborhood. Their neighbors tried to force the family to leave.

So, at a young age, Robinson learned how to stand up to bullies. He was quick to fight back when he needed to. By the time he was a teenager, Robinson had joined a gang of boys who were always in trouble.

Finally, a family friend talked to Robinson. He said, "It doesn't take guts to follow the crowd. Courage lies in being willing to be different." Robinson listened and left the gang.

All the Robinson children were athletic. Jackie's older brother Mack starred in the 1936 Olympics in Berlin. Mack finished second only to Jesse Owens in several track events.

Jackie was great at every sport he tried. At UCLA (University of California, Los Angeles), Robinson was the school's first athlete to earn varsity letters in four sports. He outscored every basketball player on the West Coast. He led the nation's college football players in rushing and punt returns. He was UCLA's best broad jumper. And he played baseball!

After college Robinson played one season of pro football for the Honolulu Bears. But then World War II broke out. Robinson was drafted.

Robinson soon found out there was racism in the army, too. When he applied for Officer Candidate School (OCS), he was turned down because of his color.

Robinson called on Joe Louis, the world heavyweight boxing champion. Louis used his clout in Washington, DC. The laws were changed to allow blacks into OCS. Robinson became a second lieutenant. He worked to change other unjust rules in the army.

After the war ended, Robinson played baseball for the Monarchs, a team in the Negro League. In 1946, Branch Rickey signed him for the

Brooklyn Dodgers farm team, the Montreal Royals. Robinson proved himself. He won the league batting title. And he won the respect of the fans and the other players.

On April 15, 1947, Robinson began playing for the Dodgers. It was not easy. Robinson received hate mail and threats to himself and his family. Fans poured abuse on him. It was constant. Robinson was angry. But he controlled himself.

Finally, his Dodger teammates began sticking up for him. The team came together, winning the National League pennant. They lost the World Series to the New York Yankees. But Jackie Robinson was named Rookie of the Year.

With his success, the door to professional baseball was opened to black players. Baseball's color barrier had fallen!

Jackie Robinson played for the Dodgers for ten years. During this time they won the National League championship six times. In 1949, Robinson won the league's Most Valuable Player award. In 1955, the Dodgers won the World Series, due mainly to Robinson's fine playing. The next year he retired. In 1962, he was elected to baseball's Hall of Fame.

Robinson became a vice president of the Chock full o'Nuts coffee company. He traveled the country speaking for the NAACP. He worked hard for civil rights with Dr. Martin Luther King Jr.

Jackie Robinson died in 1972. Robinson had said once, "A life is not important except in the impact it has on other lives." Robinson had an impact on all Americans. He was a symbol of pride and hope to black Americans. He showed white Americans that black men were worthy of respect. Jackie Robinson made a difference to all Americans.

Today Jackie Robinson's legacy lives on. The Jackie Robinson Foundation provides scholarships to black college students. And every year, April 15 is celebrated as "Jackie Robinson Day" in Major League Baseball. Robinson's uniform number 42 was retired by every team in Major League Baseball on April 15, 1997.

Remembering the Facts

1. Who decided professional baseball should be integrated?

2. How did Robinson learn to stand up to bullies?

3. Robinson was the national college champion in the broad jump. What other three sports did he excel in?

4. What ended Robinson's pro football career?

5. How did Joe Louis help Jackie Robinson?

6. What honor did Robinson win during his first season with the Dodgers?

7. What honor did Robinson get after he retired?

8. How did Robinson work for civil rights after he retired?

Understanding the Story

9.   Why do you think Branch Rickey told Robinson never to fight back when fans insulted him?

10.   Do you think Robinson's story might have ended differently if he had fought back? Explain your answer.

11.   How might it show more courage *not* to fight back than to fight back?

Getting the Main Idea

Why do you think Jackie Robinson is an important part of American history?

Applying What You've Learned

Imagine you are playing a sport. The fans are hostile and loud. How could you concentrate on your playing?

Thurgood Marshall

Supreme Court Justice

Justice Thurgood Marshall was the first African American justice on the Supreme Court. For more than 50 years he challenged America's courts to stand up for liberty and justice for all. He worked all his life for the rights of all Americans!

Thurgood Marshall was born in Baltimore in 1908. His father was a waiter at an all-white country club. His mother was a teacher in an all-black school.

Marshall's parents taught him to respect all people. They taught him to defend himself against anyone who treated him badly.

Marshall's father also taught him how to argue. The two of them could debate anything. Marshall's father taught him how to win an argument using logic and facts to prove his point. His father also took him to see courtroom trials taking place.

Marshall went to all-black schools in Baltimore. He was a bright student. But he liked to have fun, too. He liked to argue with the teachers and play tricks. So he was often in trouble.

Students who made trouble in class were sent to the basement. There they had to memorize parts of the United States Constitution. Later they had to recite what they'd learned for the class. By the time Marshall graduated from high school, he'd learned the entire Constitution by heart!

After high school, Marshall went to Lincoln University in Oxford, Pennsylvania. His mother hoped he would become a dentist. After failing biology, he decided science was not for him.

What Marshall was really good at was debating. He decided to become a lawyer. He applied to the University of Maryland School of Law. But he was turned down because of his race.

So Marshall went to Howard University, a black university. He graduated with honors in 1933. While in school, he became close friends with Charles Hamilton Houston, one of his professors.

Houston later left the university to work for the NAACP (National Associaltion for the Advancement of Colored People). He hired Thurgood Marshall as an NAACP lawyer.

In 1933, the NAACP had an important case. A young black man wanted to attend the University of Maryland School of Law. He had been turned down—just as Marshall had been a few years earlier.

Marshall and Houston fought the case in court. They argued that segregation was against the ideals that America was founded upon. They won the case!

In 1938, Thurgood Marshall became head of the NAACP's Legal Defense Fund. For the next 23 years, he fought many cases of segregation. In all, Marshall argued 32 cases before the United States Supreme Court. He won 29 of them!

Thurgood Marshall won his most important case in 1954. The name of the case was *Brown* v. *the Board of Education*. This case had to do with the segregation of children in public schools.

In Topeka, Kansas, a court had ruled that a seven-year-old black girl named Linda Brown could not attend a white school near her home. Instead, Linda had to cross dangerous railroad tracks. Then she had to catch a bus to the "colored school" across town. Linda's parents had sued the Topeka Board of Education and lost.

The United States Supreme Court agreed to hear an appeal of this ruling. Thurgood Marshall was the lawyer for Linda Brown. For three days, he argued the case before the Supreme Court.

It took the Supreme Court a whole year to make a decision. Finally, they ruled that segregated schools were against the law. This important decision opened the door for blacks to get better educations. Some states, especially in the South, did not want to obey the Court. Thurgood Marshall led the fight to make all the states and their schools obey.

President Kennedy appointed Marshall to the U.S. Court of Appeals for the Second Circuit in 1961. He was the first black to hold this job.

In 1965, President Johnson appointed Marshall Solicitor General. This meant he would represent the United States in cases being heard by the Supreme Court.

Then on June 13, 1967, President Johnson nominated Thurgood Marshall to be a justice on the Supreme Court. The United States Senate confirmed him on August 30.

Thurgood Marshall served on the Supreme Court for 24 years. He retired in 1991. He died two years later in 1993. Across the country flags were flown at half-staff. His body lay in state inside the Supreme Court chambers.

Many buildings have been named in honor of Thurgood Marshall. One of them is the law library at the University of Maryland School of Law. This is the same school that refused to admit him years earlier because he was black. In 2003, a stamp was issued honoring Thurgood Marshall and his work.

All his life, Thurgood Marshall worked to achieve justice for all. He was against the death penalty. He championed women's rights. Thurgood Marshall worked for the rights of all Americans.

Remembering the Facts

1. What skill did Marshall learn from his father?

2. How were students disciplined in Marshall's school?

3. Where did Marshall go to law school?

4. What group did Marshall begin working for in 1938?

5. What was Marshall's most important case?

6. Why was this case so important to blacks?

7. What position was Marshall appointed to in 1967?

8. Name two things Marshall worked for in his career.

Understanding the Story

9. Why couldn't black children get an equal education in segregated schools?

10. Marshall believed that racial justice could be won through the law. Do you agree? Why or why not?

Getting the Main Idea

Why do you think Thurgood Marshall is an important part of American history?

Applying What You've Learned

Imagine you are the first black student to enroll at an all-white school. What do you think might happen on your first day? How would you feel?

Rosa Parks

Civil Rights Activist

The year was 1988. The Democratic National Convention was being held in Atlanta, Georgia. Jesse Jackson, a black leader who was running for President of the United States, rose to speak. Standing beside him was a small, 75-year-old black woman named Rosa Parks. Jackson presented Parks to the cheering crowd. But everybody there already knew who she was.

Rosa Parks was the woman who had refused to give up her seat on that bus more than 30 years before. This small act of courage had set in motion the great changes in America that were to take place. Jesse Jackson knew the story. That is why he presented Parks to the crowd with just a few simple words. He said, "Rosa Parks. We all stand on her shoulders."

Rosa Parks was born Rosa McCauley on February 4, 1913 in Tuskegee, Alabama. Rosa's mother was a teacher. Her father was a carpenter. By the time Rosa was two, her father had left the family. She never saw him again during her childhood.

Rosa and her younger brother were raised by their mother and grandparents. They lived in a small house on the family farm in Pine Level, Alabama. Rosa grew up working on the farm and watching her little brother.

When Rosa turned six, she went to the black school, an old one-room building. There were 60 students of all ages in the class and only one teacher. There were no desks or windows, and almost no books. And school was only open five or six months a year. The students worked in the fields the other months.

On the way to school, Rosa walked past the new brick school for white children. This school had plenty of books and teachers. It was paid for by taxes that had been paid by both blacks and whites. And white children rode buses to school while blacks walked.

For middle school, Rosa went to the Montgomery Industrial School for Black Girls in Montgomery, Alabama. The 250 students learned academic subjects as well as sewing, cooking, and how to care for sick people. The teachers at the school were white women from the North. These women believed strongly that blacks deserved a good education. For their efforts, the teachers were treated badly by the other whites in town.

There was no public high school for blacks in Montgomery. So Rosa attended a private high school. To pay for her tuition, Rosa did cleaning and sewing. Unfortunately, Rosa had to drop out of high school. First her grandmother, then her mother, became ill. Rosa had to care for them. At the same time, she had to run the farm.

In 1931, Rosa met a barber named Raymond Parks. Two years later they were married. The couple agreed that Rosa should finish her high school education. At the age of 20, she got her diploma.

Only about 7% of blacks at that time had a high school diploma. Rosa was considered very well educated. However, this did not mean she would get a better job. Good jobs were reserved for whites. The only job Rosa could find was a low-paying job as a helper in a hospital. She also did sewing for people at her home.

Rosa and her husband became members of the NAACP. This was a group that worked for black rights. Rosa was elected secretary of the Montgomery branch. She worked in this volunteer position for 12 years. During this time, she met the leading civil rights leaders of the day.

The NAACP wanted to end segregation. They began to look for cases in which blacks were arrested for violating the Jim Crow segregation laws. One of these laws in Montgomery had to do with seating on city buses. The first four rows of seats on every city bus in Montgomery were for whites only. Blacks had to sit in the back of the bus. If the white section was filled, blacks had to get out of their seats or get off the bus to make more seating for white riders.

December 1, 1955, was a hot day in Montgomery. Rosa Parks had finished her day of doing alterations at the department store where she worked. Parks got on the bus and sat in the row of seats right behind the white section.

A few stops down the route, several white folks got on the bus. The driver yelled that all blacks in the first row would have to get up and stand in the back of the bus. The other blacks got up quietly. But Rosa Parks stayed seated. The driver repeated his order to move. "Are you going to stand up?" he asked. Parks said, "No, I'm not." The driver was angry. "I'll call the police if you don't get up," he shouted. "You may do that," Parks answered calmly.

The driver left the bus and returned with two police officers. "Why don't you stand up?" one of them asked. "Why do you push us around?" Parks answered. "I don't know," the officer stated. "But the law is the law, and you're under arrest." The 42-year-old seamstress was taken to the police station and booked.

Word of Parks' arrest spread quickly through the black community. A group of black ministers met to plan a boycott of the city bus system. They formed a group called the Montgomery Improvement Association (MIA). A 26-year-old Baptist minister named Martin Luther King Jr. was named president of the MIA.

The MIA asked blacks not to ride the buses on Monday, December 5, the day of Rosa Parks' trial. The entire black community joined in the boycott. Blacks rode to work in carpools. They rode to work in black-owned taxis that charged only the bus fare (10 cents). And over 40,000 blacks walked to work that day. Some walked as far as 20 miles.

Parks was tried and found guilty of violating the segregation laws. The trial lasted only five minutes. Parks was fined $10 plus $4 for court costs.

At a church rally that night, Martin Luther King Jr. spoke to a huge crowd. He said, "We're going to work with grim and firm determination to gain justice on the buses in this city … We are going to work and fight until justice runs down like water … We are going to work together. Right here in Montgomery, when the history books are written in the future, somebody will have to say, 'There lived a race of people, black people, … who had the moral courage to stand up for their rights.'"

After King finished speaking, every person in the hall voted to continue the boycott. No blacks would ride the city buses until the MIA's demands were met. The MIA asked that black bus riders be treated politely. They wanted blacks to be hired as bus drivers. And they wanted a new seating system. Blacks would fill seats from the back and whites from the front until all seats were taken.

Violence against blacks increased. Black churches were bombed. Martin Luther King Jr. received nightly phone calls threatening his life. His house was bombed. Luckily, King's wife and two-month-old child were able to escape unharmed.

The boycott lasted 382 days. Finally, the U.S. Supreme Court ruled that Montgomery's segregated seating on the buses was unconstitutional. On December 21, 1956, blacks rode the buses again. They could now sit wherever they wanted. But the violence continued. Shots were fired into buses and King's home. Bombs were thrown into churches and ministers' homes.

The victory had come at a high price for Rosa Parks and her husband as well. They received endless threatening phone calls. Both lost their jobs and no one would hire them. Finally, they decided to move to Detroit. Ray Parks got a job as a teacher in a barber school. Rosa took in sewing for extra money. And she continued to travel making speeches for civil rights causes. She also set up a charity to fight the poverty she found in her new neighborhood.

On August 28, 1963, Parks took part in the March on Washington. More than 250,000 people had marched to Washington in support of civil rights for all Americans. It was on this day that Martin Luther King Jr. delivered his famous "I Have a Dream" speech.

In 1964, President Lyndon B. Johnson signed the landmark civil rights bill into law. This law prohibited racial discrimination in employment and public places. It also allowed the government to withhold money from schools that refused to desegregate.

In 1964, John Conyers, a black man from Michigan, was elected to Congress. Rosa Parks supported him in his campaign. After that, she went to work for him as an office assistant. She continued working for him for the next 24 years.

Rosa Parks received many awards for her work. In 1980, she was awarded the Martin Luther King Jr. Nonviolent Peace Prize. That same year, she wa also given the Service Award from *Ebony* magazine.

But Rosa Parks' proudest achievement was the founding of the Rosa and Raymond Parks Institute for Self Development in 1987. Its Pathways to Freedom program teaches young people African-American history. It includes a bus tour to civil rights and Underground Railroad sites around the country.

In 1992, Rosa Parks wrote *Rosa Parks: My Story.* She followed this with *Quiet Strength: The Faith, the Hope, and Heart of a Woman Who Changed a Nation* in 1994.

In 1996, President Bill Clinton awarded Rosa Parks the Presidential Medal of Freedom. That same year, *Time* magazine named her one of the most influential figures of the twentieth century.

In the year 2000, the Rosa Parks Library and Museum were opened in Montgomery, Alabama, on the very corner where Rosa boarded the famed bus in 1955. That famous bus is now in the Henry Ford Museum in Michigan.

Rosa Parks died on October 24, 2005. Her body lay in honor in the U.S. Capital Rotunda. All flags in the United States flew at half-staff on the day of her funeral. And the front seats of all buses in Montgomery, Alabama, had black ribbons in her honor.

Today, The Rosa Parks Institute continues the work she began. As Parks said in *Quiet Strength*, "There is work to do. That is why I cannot stop or sit still. As long as a child needs help, as long as people are not free, there will be work to do."

Remembering the Facts

1. Why did Rosa Parks work at a low-paying job even though she was well educated?

2. Why was Rosa Parks 20 years old when she received her high school diploma?

3. What did blacks have to do if there weren't enough seats for white bus riders?

4. Name two demands of the MIA.

5. How did whites react to the bus boycott?

6. Why did Rosa Parks and her husband move to Detroit?

7. What is the purpose of the Rosa and Raymond Parks Institute for Self Development?

Understanding the Story

8. What do you think Jesse Jackson meant when he said, "Rosa Parks. We all stand on her shoulders"?

9. Why do you think only 7% of blacks in the 1950s had a high school diploma?

10. Why do you think seating on the buses was such a big issue to blacks?

Getting the Main Idea

Why do you think Rosa Parks is an important part of American history?

Applying What You've Learned

Imagine that Rosa Parks is speaking in your school. Write an introduction describing her accomplishments and the impact she made on the civil rights movement.

Dr. Martin Luther King Jr.

Civil Rights Leader

If you're thirsty, you can drink from any water fountain. If you're hungry, you can go into any restaurant and eat. If you need a ride, you can get on a train or bus and sit anywhere you want. But if you were black and lived in the South before 1960, you would not have had any of these rights.

From the end of the Civil War until the late 1950s, African Americans were segregated from white people by Jim Crow laws in all the southern states.

In public places there were signs reading "Whites Only." Blacks could not go to school with whites. They had to ride in the backs of buses. And they could use only the water fountains and restrooms marked "Colored." Any black person who did not obey could be arrested.

Protest against this unfair treatment grew in the late 1950s. The leader of this civil rights movement was Dr. Martin Luther King Jr. King was born on January 15, 1929. His father was the minister of Atlanta's Ebenezer Baptist Church. As a boy, King loved to listen to his father's preaching. "When I grow up, I'm going to get me some big words, too," he said.

King's parents taught him that all men are created equal. But at an early age, he found out that a lot of people didn't think that way. King grew up with prejudice all around him.

King was a gifted student. At age 15, he graduated from high school. He went on to Morehouse College. While there, he decided to become a minister like his father.

After graduating from Morehouse, King went on to Crozer Seminary in Chester, Pennsylvania. Here, for the first time, he was free from the Jim Crow laws.

While at Crozer, King studied the life of Mahatma Gandhi. Gandhi had led a revolution that freed the native people of India from English rule. Gandhi called his protest method "passive resistance."

Gandhi said that if laws were unfair, people should not obey them. If arrested for breaking an unjust law, people should go to jail without protest. Gandhi believed that no one should use violence to protest injustice. He knew that love was the most powerful weapon against hatred. King was later to use these same methods in the civil rights movement.

After graduating from seminary, King went on to Boston University School of Theology. He earned a doctorate degree, the highest academic degree.

King met Coretta Scott in Boston. On their first date, King told her she was everything he was looking for in a wife. In 1953, they were married.

In 1954, King was offered a job as pastor of the Dexter Avenue Baptist Church in Montgomery, Alabama. He had two other job offers in northern churches. It was a hard decision. He and Coretta did not really want to move back to the South.

But the Supreme Court had just ruled that all schools should be open to both blacks and whites. King knew this could be the beginning of big changes for blacks. He wanted to be a part of it. So he moved back to the deep South.

In Montgomery, Alabama, blacks were forced to sit in the backs of buses. If a bus got full, blacks had to give up their seats for whites.

On December 1, 1955, a black woman named Rosa Parks got on a city bus. When the driver told her to give up her seat to a white man, she refused. Rosa Parks was put in jail.

Blacks were angry. They decided to boycott (not use) the buses. King spoke to a large group of them. "We must use the weapon of protest," he said. "But we must protest with courage, dignity, and Christian love." Twenty-seven-year-old King became the spokesman for the boycott.

The boycott was a huge success. When news of the boycott reached the outside world, it exposed the racial problems in the South. Finally, on November 13, 1956, the U.S. Supreme Court ruled that the Montgomery buses must be desegregated. Gandhi's method of nonviolent protest had won!

Southern black ministers formed a group called the Southern Christian Leadership Conference (SCLC). King was elected leader of the group. The SCLC planned peaceful protests all over the South.

On February 1, 1960, four young black men sat down at a lunch counter in Greensboro, North Carolina. They politely asked for some coffee. They were refused. So they sat there quietly until the store closed. The SCLC encouraged "sit-ins" like this at lunch counters all over the country. Again the world watched these events on TV.

King and the other SCLC leaders decided to stage a protest march in Birmingham, Alabama. While leading the march, King was arrested and put in jail. There King wrote his famous "Letter from a Birmingham Jail." His letter told why the time to fight against racism was now. This letter was read by people around the world.

When King got out of jail, he led a children's march through the streets of Birmingham. A thousand children, some as young as six, were arrested and put in jail. The next day 2,500 children marched. Police attacked them with dogs and sprayed them with firehoses. People everywhere were outraged!

President John F. Kennedy was angry, too. He went on TV and told all Americans that segregation must end. He said he would ask Congress to pass a law giving all Americans the right to be served in public places. On June 19, 1963, Kennedy sent the civil rights bill to Congress.

King and other black leaders wanted to be sure the bill was made law. So they organized a huge march on Washington, DC. Over 250,000 people, many of them white, came to Washington on "freedom trains" and "freedom buses."

King gave his "I Have a Dream" speech in front of the Lincoln Memorial. The speech told of his dream that blacks and whites could live together in peace. "I have a dream," he said, "that my four little children will one day live in a nation where they will not be judged by the color of their skin, but by the content of their character.... Let freedom ring!"

Finally, on July 2, 1964, the Civil Rights Act became law. Soon after that, King was awarded the Nobel Peace Prize. This award is given to the person who has done the most to further peace for that year.

King seemed to know he would not live a long life. The night before his death, King said, "It doesn't matter what happens to me. I've been to the mountaintop. I've seen the Promised Land. I may not get there with you. But we as a people will get there."

The next day on April 4, 1968, he was in Memphis. He stepped out onto the balcony of his motel room for some fresh air. Suddenly a shot rang out. King fell to the floor dead. He was only 39 years old. The killer was a man named James Earl Ray.

The news of King's death sparked riots in over 100 cities. People around the world mourned his death. Over 100,000 people walked sadly in King's last march for freedom.

In 1986, the birthday of Dr. Martin Luther King Jr. became a national holiday. Martin Luther King Day is celebrated on January 15. On this day we remember his dream that we would all live together in peace and freedom.

Remembering the Facts

1. What were Jim Crow laws?

2. What did King learn from studying the life of Gandhi?

3. Why did King decide to return to the South after he finished his studies?

4. What group of ministers planned protests all over the South?

5. What was the purpose of the huge march on Washington, DC, in 1963?

6. What was the main idea of King's "I Have a Dream" speech?

7. What award did King receive in 1964?

Understanding the Story

8. Why do you think television helped the cause of civil rights?

9. After King's death, riots took place across the country. What do you think King would have said about this? Why?

10. Many blacks fought for freedom and civil rights over the years. Why do you think it is Martin Luther King Jr. whose birthday is remembered?

Getting the Main Idea

Why do you think Dr. Martin Luther King Jr. is an important part of American history?

Applying What You've Learned

Imagine you are a black teenager living in the deep South in the 1950s. How do you think the Jim Crow laws would affect your life? Explain how you think you would feel about them.

Malcolm X

Black Militant Leader

Not all black leaders in the 1950s and 60s agreed with Dr. Martin Luther King's ideas of nonviolence. Malcolm X was the most outspoken of King's opponents.

Malcolm X did not want to be "brothers" with whites. He did not think integration would work either. He wanted blacks to form their own nation.

Malcolm X felt that blacks needed economic power. He encouraged blacks to help one another. They should build their own businesses. They should do business with one another. And they should build their own schools.

Malcolm X thought that progress in the racial struggle was too slow. He thought blacks should take their civil rights, using force if needed. He called for a "revolution" to cut ties with the United States and form a black nation. This country could be either within the United States or in Africa. Malcolm X's ideas scared white people and most blacks, as well.

Malcolm X was born Malcolm Little in Omaha, Nebraska in 1925. His father was a Baptist minister. He preached militant ideas, too.

Malcolm grew up in violent times. Three of his uncles were lynched by the Ku Klux Klan. His father was threatened. So the family moved to East Lansing, Michigan, hoping to be safe.

Malcolm's father kept preaching. When Malcolm was four, the Klan set fire to his home as the family slept. They escaped just as the house fell down around them.

16 Extraordinary African Americans

Yet Malcolm's father kept preaching. When Malcolm was six, the Klan killed his father by throwing him under a trolley car. By the age of six, Malcolm knew more about violence and death than any child should ever know.

Malcolm got good grades in school. But after finishing eighth grade, he dropped out. He lived on the streets and began a life of crime. A few months after his 21st birthday, he went to prison for ten years for burglary.

Malcolm later said, "I finished the eighth grade at Mason Junior High. My high school was the black ghetto. My college was the streets of Harlem. And my master's degree was taken in prison."

It was prison that finally turned Malcolm's life around. While there, he learned about the Black Muslim religion.

Black Muslims taught black pride. They believed in strong families. They did not allow the use of tobacco, drugs, or alcohol.

The Black Muslims also stressed education. Malcolm began attending the prison school. He read everything he could find, including the dictionary and a complete set of encyclopedias.

After he got out of prison, Malcolm joined the Black Muslims. When he did, he changed his name. "Little" had been the name of the white family that once owned Malcolm's ancestors. So he called himself Malcolm X.

In 1958, Malcolm X married Betty X. (She was later known as Betty Shabazz.) The couple had six daughters.

Malcolm X went to Chicago to meet Elijah Muhammad, the leader of the Black Muslims. It did not take long before Malcolm X had become second in command to Muhammad. He also published a newspaper called *Muhammad Speaks*.

For 12 years, Malcolm X preached the Black Muslim message. He organized scores of temples across the country. He spoke for black rights and freedom. Then, in 1963, Malcolm X split from Muhammad's group. He formed a new group called Muslim Mosque. This was to be a revolutionary group.

In 1964, Malcolm X traveled to Mecca, the holy city for Muslims. There he changed his views on race.

In Mecca, he saw Muslims of every race living together in peace and love. He saw "people of all races, colors, from all over the world coming together as one!" From that time on, he stopped judging people by their skin color.

By 1965, Malcolm X had become afraid for his life. Many of his followers had been beaten. He had received death threats. His house was firebombed.

But Malcolm X did not stop preaching his ideas. He also kept working on the story of his life, *The Autobiography of Malcolm X*. He hoped his book would spread his views.

On February 21, 1965, Malcolm was giving a speech at the Audubon Ballroom in Harlem. Three men rushed forward and shot him. One man was caught; the other two fled. To this day, no one knows who planned the murder.

In the 1960s, Malcolm X was feared as a black militant. Over the years, his contributions have become respected. His picture is on a U.S. postage stamp. By many he is thought of as a leader of equal importance to Martin Luther King Jr. Indeed, as Malcolm X once said, "Dr. King wants the same thing I want—freedom!"

Many of Malcolm X's ideas live on. To many, he is a symbol of black manhood, black pride, and black power. He stands for blacks looking to their African culture and heritage. Malcolm X has had a lasting impact on American history.

Remembering the Facts

1. Where and when was Malcolm X born?

2. Name two violent episodes Malcolm X faced as a child.

3. How did Malcolm X gain direction in prison?

4. Name three teachings of the Black Muslims.

5. Why did Malcolm X change his last name?

6. How were Malcolm X's views different from Dr. King's?

7. How did Malcolm X soften his views in Mecca?

8. What ideas of Malcolm X live on today?

Understanding the Story

9.   Why do you think many people were frightened by Malcolm X's ideas?

10.   How do you think his father influenced Malcolm X's life?

Getting the Main Idea

Why do you think Malcolm X is an important part of American history?

Applying What You've Learned

Imagine that you are a black teenager in 1964. Your family is poor and on welfare. You go to hear Malcolm X speak. What do you think of his ideas? Why?

Jesse Jackson

Rainbow Coalition Leader

It was a hot night in Atlanta, Georgia. The 1988 Democratic National Convention was meeting for its final night. Jesse Jackson had won 30% of the delegates to the convention. But it was not enough. He had lost the nomination for President of the United States.

Now thousands were waiting to listen to Jesse Jackson. Finally, he rose to speak.

"Dr. Martin Luther King Jr. lies only a few miles from us tonight," he said. "Tonight he must feel good as he looks down upon us. We sit here together, a rainbow coalition, the sons and daughters of slavemasters, and the sons and daughters of slaves. We sit around a common table to decide the direction of our party and our country." Jackson's stirring speech received a 15-minute standing ovation.

Jackson had run a historic race for president. His backers were called the Rainbow Coalition. As Jackson put it, "red and yellow and brown and black and white" people supported him. He inspired people of all races.

Jesse Louis Jackson was born in Greenville, South Carolina, in 1941 to an unmarried high school student. His family was poor. So Jesse worked many jobs as a boy. He shined shoes. He waited tables. He worked at a lumberyard. He was a golf caddy.

In high school, Jesse was an outstanding athlete. He excelled in football, basketball, and baseball.

Jesse graduated from high school in 1959. He went to the University of Illinois on a football scholarship. Jackson had been a star quarterback in high school. He hoped to do the same in college. But the coach told him that all black football players on the team had to be linemen.

The next year, Jesse transferred to all-black North Carolina A & T College. There he was a star quarterback. He was also an honor student and president of the student body.

In 1963, Jesse led the A & T College civil rights movement. He started daily sit-ins in Greensboro businesses that refused to serve blacks. Jackson forced Greensboro to drop its segregation laws. He gained national fame for his work.

While leading the sit-ins, Jackson met Jacqueline Davis. They later married and had five children.

Jackson wanted to be a leader in the civil rights struggle. He knew that ministers were the most respected leaders in the black community. So he went to the Chicago Theological Seminary.

Jackson soon found that Chicago was very different from the South. There were no segregation laws. But most blacks were poor and out of work. They lived in crowded old apartment buildings that were full of rats. This part of town was called the black ghetto.

In the ghetto, the stores were owned by whites. Prices were high. Blacks shopped in these stores because it was hard for them to go anywhere else. Not only that, these white-owned stores did not hire many black workers.

Jackson wanted to make things better. He got that chance in 1966. Dr. Martin Luther King Jr. asked him to head Chicago's Operation Breadbasket.

Operation Breadbasket had two goals. It helped black-owned businesses. And it worked to get white-owned businesses to hire black workers.

To reach these goals, Jackson set up boycotts. Blacks refused to buy from the ghetto stores. They would not buy products made by companies that hired no black workers. Stores were soon forced to hire black workers or go out of business.

In 1967, Jackson was made the national head of Operation Breadbasket. He gained thousands of jobs and business opportunities for black workers.

A year later, Jackson became a Baptist minister. Thousands heard his sermons over the radio.

Reverend Jackson appealed to young African Americans. He dressed and wore his hair the way they did. But more than that, he spoke their language.

"I am somebody!" he would call out. "I am somebody," the people would answer. "I am black, beautiful, proud," he would go on. "I am black, beautiful, proud," answered the crowd. "I may be black, I may be poor, I may have lost hope, but I am God's child." Jackson's message brought pride to many black youth.

On April 4, 1968, Jackson was working with Dr. King in Memphis. That evening King was shot. Jackson was with King when he died.

In 1971, Jackson started Operation PUSH (People United to Save Humanity). PUSH worked to help black-owned businesses. PUSH talked many huge national companies into hiring more blacks. During the next 15 years, PUSH spread to 16 major cities.

Jackson traveled across the country speaking about the goals of PUSH. He told people that the fight was not over. Blacks had won their civil rights. Now they must work for better jobs and a better way of life.

Jackson was upset by what he saw in many inner-city schools. He spoke at hundreds of schools trying to get students to stay in school and study. His message was anti-drug, too. "Say no to drugs, say yes to life," he urged.

In 1984, Jackson ran for president of the United States. He won only one primary. The Democratic nomination went to Walter Mondale. But Jackson had proved to be the leading African-American politician of his day.

In 1988, he ran again. This time people took him more seriously. Whites and blacks jumped on the Jackson bandwagon. This time he came much closer to winning the Democratic nomination.

In 1997, PUSH and the Rainbow Coalition merged. The new group is known as RainbowPUSH Coalition. Its goals are to protect civil rights. It works for equal opportunities in business and education. It also strives to bring peace to the world.

Jackson continues to work for social change. He hopes to make the American dream come true for everyone. Jackson has said, "The American Dream is one big tent of many cultures, races, and religions. Under that tent, everyone is assured … a fair share. Our struggle demands that we open closed doors … and level the playing field."

Jackson is concerned about the rise in violent crime in the United States. He warns that black-on-black crime is destroying many of the gains made by the civil rights movement. He calls for all Americans to take the "moral offensive against violence."

Jackson travels the world and works for civil rights. In 2004, he tried to bring peace to Northern Ireland. In 2005, he worked to register more black voters in England.

Jesse Jackson has been the most influential African-American leader since Martin Luther King. Under his leadership, the fight for freedom goes on.

Remembering the Facts

1.   Why was Jesse Jackson's 1988 race for president important?

2.   How did Jackson win fame in Greensboro, South Carolina?

3.   How was life for blacks in Chicago different from Greensboro in the 1960s?

4.   What was the purpose of Operation Breadbasket?

5.   What was the Rainbow Coalition?

6.   Explain a goal of the RainbowPUSH Coalition.

7.   How has Jackson expanded his fight around the world?

Understanding the Story

8.   Many white-owned stores in the ghetto charged high prices. Why do you think blacks shopped at these stores?

9.   Why do you think it was hard for African Americans to open their own stores?

10.   Jesse Jackson was inspired by Dr. Martin Luther King Jr. How is Jackson's lifework similar to that of Dr. King?

Getting the Main Idea

Why do you think Jesse Jackson is an important part of American history?

Applying What You've Learned

Imagine that a company in your town refused to do business with students. Using nonviolent tactics, how could you get this company to change its ways?

Maya Angelou

Poet Laureate

Maya Angelou's poem "On the Pulse of Morning" was heard by millions of Americans at President Clinton's inauguration. The poem is Angelou's vision of hope for the future of our country. Here is a part of that poem:

> "Lift up your eyes upon
> This day breaking for you.
>
> Give birth again
> To the dream....
>
> Here, on the pulse of this new day
> You may have the grace to look up
>   and out
> And into your sister's eyes, and into
> Your brother's face, your country
> And say simply
> Very simply
> With hope—
> Good morning."

Maya Angelou was born in St. Louis, Missouri, in 1928. When she was three, her parents divorced. She and her four-year-old brother, Bailey, were put on a train. They traveled all the way to Stamps, Arkansas, by themselves to live with their grandmother.

Their grandmother, "Momma," owned a store in the black part of town. It was during the Depression, and they were poor. But Momma kept her family together. Momma was a religious woman. She taught Maya that she could control her future with hard work and courage.

Maya's grandmother taught her to love reading. She read the works of many black authors. Maya was kept sheltered from a world in which blacks were treated unfairly. She learned to stay away from whites. She later said that white people were not real to her as a child. She thought that if you touched one, "your hand would go right through them."

When Maya was seven, she and her brother went back to live with their mother. Their mother worked as a blues singer and as a dealer in a gambling parlor.

At the age of eight, Maya was raped by her mother's boyfriend. He was tried and found guilty. When he was let out of jail, an angry mob attacked him and kicked him to death.

For safety, Maya and her brother returned to Stamps. But the horror of the rape would not leave Maya alone. She did not speak for five years. It was during this time that she began writing poetry.

Maya graduated from the eighth grade at the top of her class. Then she and Bailey went back to live with their mother in San Francisco. Maya went to high school. She took drama and dance lessons.

During the next few years she had many different jobs. She was a cook, a cocktail waitress, a streetcar conductor, and a dancer. She became an unwed mother at sixteen. She experimented with drugs. She also lived in Africa for a while.

Later she married a man named Tosh Angelos. The marriage did not last long. To support her son, Maya got a job as a dancer.

Performers from the famous Purple Onion nightclub saw Maya dance and offered her a job. Maya found success as a singer and dancer. She performed all over the United States and Europe.

By the time she was 30, Maya had decided to become a writer. She wrote the first book of her autobiography, *I Know Why the Caged Bird Sings,* in 1969. This was followed by five more books of autobiography. She has also written a number of volumes of poetry. In 2002, she wrote *A Song Flung Up to Heaven.* This book completed the six books of autobiography she started 33 years earlier.

Her message in all these works is the same. "You may have many defeats. But you must not be defeated." She says that failures can help you learn who you are.

In 1981, Maya was awarded a lifetime chair as the Reynolds Professor of American Studies at Wake Forest University in North Carolina. She teaches and travels across the country giving speeches.

A highlight of Maya's career came when President Clinton asked her to write a poem for his inauguration. The poem she wrote is "On the Pulse of Morning."

The theme of the poem is one that is found in all her works. Maya celebrates the human spirit. She believes that all humans are more alike than they are unlike. She is filled with hope for the future of our country. She loves life!

Maya Angelou is our nation's poet laureate. She is only the second poet laureate in our nation's history. The first was Robert Frost, who presented a poem at the inauguration of President John F. Kennedy.

Today, Maya Angelou is viewed as one of the greatest American writers. In all her writing, she shows her courage as a black woman. She has not been defeated by her problems. She rises above them. As she tells her own life story, she also tells of the struggle of all blacks against racism. Maya has lived the theme of her writing: the triumph of the human spirit over adversity.

Remembering the Facts

1. What poem did Maya Angelou write for President Clinton's inauguration?

2. How did Maya's grandmother influence her?

3. When did Maya begin writing poetry?

4. Name three jobs Maya held as a young woman.

5. What is the name of Maya's first book of autobiography?

6. What poet read at the inauguration of John F. Kennedy?

7. Describe the main theme in all of Maya's writings.

Understanding the Story

8. Maya says, "You may have many defeats. But you must not be defeated." How has she lived this ideal in her own life?

9. Why do you think President Clinton chose Maya Angelou to give her message to the country on his Inauguration Day?

10. Maya says, "As human beings we are more alike than unlike." What do you think this means?

Getting the Main Idea

Why do you think Maya Angelou is an important part of American history?

Applying What You've Learned

Write a poem expressing an idea that is important in your own life.

Toni Morrison

Author

The Nobel Prize for Literature is the most important writing award in the world. Toni Morrison was the first black woman to win it. The prize that year was worth $825,000. But more important to Morrison was the fact that she was now known around the world as a great writer.

Toni Morrison was born as Chloe Anthony Wofford on February 18, 1931. She was the second of four children. She grew up in Lorain, Ohio. Lorain is a small factory town 25 miles west of Cleveland.

Chloe's father worked hard to support his family. Sometimes he worked three jobs at a time. His best job was as a shipyard welder. He took great pride in his work. If he welded a seam perfectly, he signed it. No one would ever see his name, but he would know it was there. From her father, Chloe learned how important it was to work hard and pay attention to details.

The Woffords were a close-knit family. The things they enjoyed most were reading and telling stories. Chloe especially loved her father's stories. He told of Uncle Remus, ghosts, magic, and the supernatural. These stories sparked young Chloe's imagination. When Chloe entered first grade, she was the only black in her class. She was also the only child who could read.

Chloe graduated from high school with honors. She went on to Howard University, a black college. Chloe found that her English professors taught only the works of white authors and ignored black writers.

Chloe had already read the books included in her courses. She was bored with campus social life. Her classmates seemed only interested in clothes and parties. She found that her classmates couldn't even say her name right. So she started using a short form of her middle name: Toni.

Toni joined an acting group called the Howard University Players. The Players put on plays throughout the Southern states. By traveling with this group, Toni got a chance to see people and places different from those she knew. She learned about racism and how it affected black people. She found that it affected white people as well. Later she would use things she learned on these trips in her writing.

Toni earned a bachelor's degree in English from Howard. In 1955, she got her master's degree in English from Cornell. She met Harold Morrison. They were married a year later. Now her name was Toni Morrison. Toni and her husband had two sons. But their marriage was not a happy one. It ended in divorce.

In 1965, Random House Publisher in New York hired Toni as an editor. She moved there with her two small sons. Every night as her sons slept, Toni wrote. At first it was just something to do. Soon it became more important to her than her paying job. She later said, "Writing became the one thing I had no intention of living without."

In 1967, Toni became a senior editor at Random House. She began editing books by famous black writers. She helped them get published. She brought a number of black authors into the mainstream of American literature.

At the same time, she kept working on her own book. When it was finished, she sent it to many publishers. In 1970, *The Bluest Eye* was published. It did not sell many copies. But the reviewers agreed that it was an amazing first novel. *The Bluest Eye* tells the story of a young black girl who believes that all her problems would go away if only she had blue eyes.

Toni wrote her next book in her head on her daily subway ride. *Sula*, the story of the friendship of two black women, was published in 1975. *Sula* got good reviews. But it did not sell many copies. So Toni decided not to write another novel.

She had an idea for a book about African-American history. It was a scrapbook that would cover 300 years of black history. It included old newspaper stories and photos. It had lyrics to songs and old stories. It had records from the patent office and ads. *The Black Book* was published in 1974.

In 1977, her third novel, *Song of Solomon*, was published. The book won the National Book Critics Circle Award in 1977. It sold many copies. With the money she made from the book, Toni bought a house on the Hudson River in New York. She worked at Random House only one day a week. She spent the rest of her time writing.

Toni spent four and a half years writing her fourth novel, *Tar Baby*. It was based on the old Uncle Remus tale of Brer Rabbit and the Tar Baby. In the book, she talked about the conflicts between the races. *Tar Baby* received mixed reviews. But it made the *New York Times* best seller list.

Toni wanted to write her next novel about slavery. She had seen an 1856 newspaper story that gave her the idea for a novel. The article told the story of an escaped slave named Margaret Garner. When her owner found her, Margaret killed her daughter Beloved rather than allowing her to return to slavery. The dead child was reincarnated (reborn) in the body of a young woman. Beloved shared her memories and those who lived before her. She shared the stories of Africans who died on the slave ships coming to America.

Beloved was a best seller. Toni's powerful writing showed the horror of the slaves' lives. For the first time, many people realized just how horrible slavery really was. In 1988, Toni received the Pulitzer Prize for *Beloved*. In May 2006, *The New York Times* Book Review named *Beloved* the best American novel written in the previous 25 years.

But Toni felt that *Beloved* told only part of the story she wanted to tell. Two more books would be needed to finish it. These books were *Jazz* (1992) and *Paradise* (1998).

On October 7, 1993, Toni learned that she had won the 1993 Nobel Prize for Literature. She was only the eleventh American to do so, and the first African-American. The Swedish Academy, which gives the prize, praised Toni's six novels for their "epic power." They spoke of her "ear for dialogue and richly expressive depictions of black America."

Toni expressed her thanks. "I am (so) happy. But what is most wonderful for me is to know that the prize at last has been awarded to an African American." Two months later, Morrison traveled to Stockholm, Sweden, to accept the prize. She hoped that her success would inspire other young black writers.

Today, Toni Morrison continues her writing. In 2003, *Love* was published. And she has also published a number of children's books with her son, Slade Morrison.

Toni Morrison is known around the world. She has received countless awards and has become wealthy from her work. But fame and money were never her goals. She once said, "There's a difference between writing for a living and writing for life." She writes because she could not live without writing.

Remembering the Facts

1. What is the name of the important writing award Toni Morrison won in 1993?

2. How did Toni get her love of telling stories?

3. Why was Toni not satisfied with her English courses at Howard?

4. Explain two ways the Howard University Players expanded Toni's horizons.

5. How did Toni use her position as an editor at Random House to help other black writers?

6. What is *Beloved* about?

7. Name the two books that completed the story Toni began in *Beloved.*

Understanding the Story

8. Why do you think *The New York Times* Book Review named *Beloved* the best American novel written in the previous 25 years?

16 Extraordinary African Americans

9. What do you think Toni meant when she said, "There's a difference between writing for a living and writing for life."

10. The library in Lorain, Ohio, recently dedicated a Toni Morrison Reading Room. Why do you think this is such a fitting honor for Toni?

Getting the Main Idea

Why do you think that Toni Morrison is an important part of American history?

Applying What You've Learned

Toni Morrison once said, "If you study the culture and art of African Americans, you are not studying a … minor culture. What you are studying is America." What do you think she meant?

Vocabulary

Sojourner Truth

protest	civil rights	Civil War
sojourner	narrative	abuse
freedman	Quakers	

Frederick Douglass

abolitionist	ambassador
slave-breaker	U.S. Marshal
plantation	

Harriet Tubman

route	overseer	seizure
indigent	devotion	heroic

Ida B. Wells-Barnett

yellow fever	injustice	verdict
appealed	militant	lynched
crusade	NAACP	

Mary McLeod Bethune

poverty	cabinet	federal agency	institute
seminary	siblings	channel	unemployment
determination	missionary	scholarship	legacy

Booker T. Washington

exposition	humanity	segregated	caste
industrial school	compromise	*Webster's Speller*	
spokesperson	legislature	donations	

W.E.B. DuBois

scholar	devote
ignorance	Ph.D.
racism	prejudice

George Washington Carver

agriculture	extraordinary	botany
crop rotation	compost heap	organic farming
imported	lapel	

Jackie Robinson

major league	athlete
Officer Candidate School	Olympics
professional	impact

Thurgood Marshall

justice	Supreme Court
logic	Constitution
nominated	debate

Rosa Parks

convention	discrimination	seamstress	desegregate
diploma	volunteer	boycott	influential
segregation	poll	unconstitutional	

Dr. Martin Luther King Jr.

Jim Crow laws	sit-in	desegregated	nonviolence
passive resistance	segregated	Nobel Peace Prize	mourned
obscene	doctorate	revolution	

Malcolm X

integration	autobiography
economic	Black Muslim
Ku Klux Klan	ghetto

Jesse Jackson

Rainbow Coalition	inspired
primary	politician
delegates	nomination

Maya Angelou

pulse	Depression
adversity	poet laureate
inauguration	

Toni Morrison

Nobel Prize	integrated
supernatural	racism

Answer Key

Sojourner Truth

Remembering the Facts

1. She gave her a strong faith in God.

2. Dumont had broken his promise to free her.

3. Quakers did not believe in slavery.

4. It was one of the first times a black person had sued a white person in court and won.

5. Sojourner said that God told her to take the name Sojourner. She herself thought of the name Truth.

6. women and blacks

7. She worked to improve conditions in the freedman's camps. She worked at the Freedman's Hospital.

Understanding the Story

8. Women in those days had very few rights. They could not vote. A married woman gave her husband all her property. Women had few opportunities for education or professional work.

9. Sojourner Truth was a unique and powerful character. She created a stir wherever she went. She was physically striking. Six feet tall, large-boned and plainly dressed, she stood out in a crowd. She had a powerful singing voice.

10. Her message was plain and blunt.

11. The freedmen had many problems. Many lived in deplorable conditions. Others were discriminated against and not allowed their rights.

Getting the Main Idea

Sojourner Truth was an abolitionist, a women's rights leader, and a religious leader. Many people of her time, especially in the North, were profoundly influenced by her speeches. She traveled over a large part of the United States and was heard by thousands of people.

Applying What You've Learned

She might have thanked him for freeing the slaves. She would have reminded him of the problems still faced by freedmen (former slaves). She would have shared her ideas for how these problems could be solved.

Frederick Douglass

Remembering the Facts

1. He was sent to work in the plantation house where they had been sent when he was a baby.

2. They were not given enough food, heat, or clothing.

3. Douglass, as a slave who could read, might not obey his master.

4. He would not act like a slave. He would not obey his master.

5. He dressed as a sailor, borrowed papers from a friend, and borrowed money for a train ticket.

6. Runaway slaves followed the North Star to freedom.

7. Any of the following: U.S. Ambassador to Haiti, U.S. Marshal for the District of Columbia, Recorder of Deeds for Washington, DC

Understanding the Story

8. The mothers were returned to work as soon as possible. Old women who couldn't work the fields cared for the children. This also prevented strong bonds from forming between mothers and children.

9. Slaves who could read could think for themselves and might not obey without question. Slaves who could read might forge papers for themselves and escape.

10. Slavery was a brutal life for the slave, but it poisoned the owner's soul as well. Owners became hardened to the suffering of the slaves. They often became cruel and almost inhuman.

Getting the Main Idea

Frederick Douglass is important because through his powerful speeches and writing, he was able to convince many people that slavery was wrong.

Applying What You've Learned

Students should mention hardships and demands placed on a slave.

Harriet Tubman

Remembering the Facts

1. She worked in the field, plowing, chopping wood, and hoeing weeds.

2. She tried to protect another slave and was hit in the head. After this, she had seizures in which she suddenly fell asleep.

3. She heard that her master planned to sell her to someone in the South.

4. about nineteen

5. the movement to free the slaves

6. Any of the following: a spy, a nurse, and a scout

7. Any of the following: raised money for schools for former slaves, collected clothing for the poor, cared for her aged parents, opened a home for elderly poor blacks

Understanding the Story

8. The idea of the Underground Railroad is romantic, suitable for legend or myth. In reality, it was dangerous and difficult work.

9. She made freeing the slaves her life's work.

10. She felt that women, in addition to blacks, had no rights and were essentially enslaved to their husbands.

Getting the Main Idea

She is a symbol of the human desire for freedom.

Applying What You've Learned

Students should include several dangers encountered. They should describe their feelings during the day's journey.

Ida B. Wells-Barnett

Remembering the Facts

1. The conductor did not want her to sit in the first-class section, which was reserved for whites.

2. She had to pay back the $500 she won in the first lawsuit plus court costs.

3. A newspaper asked her to write about her experience on the train.

4. lynching of blacks

5. "No More Lynching!"

6. NAACP

7. to provide low-cost housing and an employment center for homeless African Americans

8. They named a housing project after her.

Understanding the Story

9. White newspapers did not print much news about blacks. Also, black papers acted as an educational tool, informing African Americans about important issues of their times.

10. She would probably write about all the violence in our society and in our schools. She would have some ideas for stopping it.

Getting the Main Idea

She was very influential in stopping much of the lynching going on in the South. She helped form the NAACP.

Applying What You've Learned

Students' articles should identify both a problem and a solution for that problem.

Mary McLeod Bethune

Remembering the Facts

1. education

2. Only whites were allowed to become missionaries.

3. Many workers had gone there to work on the new railroad, and there were no schools for their children.

4. Any three of the following: baked and sold pies, put on musical performances, worked in the community, found used items from the town dump, raised funds from wealthier residents

5. Bethune-Cookman College

6. to advise President Franklin D. Roosevelt on matters affecting blacks

7. Any three of the following: love, hope, a thirst for education, faith, dignity, the desire to live in harmony with others

Understanding the Story

8. She had many friends, many of them powerful and well-educated. She made Bethune-Cookman College a success. She was able to influence President Roosevelt to put money into black education and jobs.

9. She started with very little but had faith she could succeed. She built Bethune-Cookman College from nothing to a large school. She had little formal education but became advisor to a president. She relentlessly pursued her goals.

10. Bethune worked hard all her life to better those less fortunate than herself. She kept very little for herself.

Getting the Main Idea

She advanced educational opportunities for African Americans. She was the first black woman to head a federal agency. She was a close advisor to Franklin D. Roosevelt.

Applying What You've Learned

Students should discuss how they could live their lives according to the ideals she lists in her legacy.

Booker T. Washington

Remembering the Facts

1. the Atlanta Compromise

2. He said they should wait for their civil rights until they became better educated.

3. the Hampton Institute

4. the Tuskegee Institute

5. The Alabama legislature paid the teachers. He got donations for the rest.

6. They thought blacks should get equal civil rights immediately.

7. Theodore Roosevelt and Grover Cleveland

Understanding the Story

8. Whites liked the idea of blacks being second-class citizens and staying "in their place." They liked the idea of blacks learning trades and serving whites. They especially liked the idea of blacks and whites being separate.

9. He thought African Americans should learn skills they could put to immediate use.

10. The fingers on the hand are separate. But they can work together to accomplish a common goal. Whites used this story to justify segregation or separate facilities for blacks.

Getting the Main Idea

For many years, Booker T. Washington was the spokesperson for the black race. His successful Tuskegee Institute provided an opportunity for African Americans to further their education. Because whites listened to him, Washington was able to secure gains for blacks in some areas.

Applying What You've Learned

Students should mention earning a living, finding housing, educating themselves, feeding and clothing themselves, etc.

W.E.B. DuBois

Remembering the Facts

1. His parents had never been slaves. He lived in a small town and faced little discrimination. He was able to associate with the best families because of his intellectual ability.

2. Attending Fisk University put him in the South for the first time. Teaching in a rural school made him aware of the lifestyle of poor black sharecroppers.

3. *The Souls of Black Folk* explains why educated blacks (the "talented tenth") must lead the others to a better life.

4. NAACP

5. He wanted to be prepared to be a leader.

6. Ghana, West Africa

7. a study of African blacks

Understanding the Story

8. He meant that the racial problem was the most important issue facing America.

9. Answers will vary.

10. DuBois felt that blacks should not passively accept second-class citizenship. He felt that blacks would never gain their civil rights under Washington's programs.

Getting the Main Idea

DuBois was the link between two great African-American leaders: Frederick Douglass and Dr. Martin Luther King Jr. DuBois gave modern civil rights workers the base from which they started. Also, he showed the importance of education and hard work to black progress.

Applying What You've Learned

He felt that those who were blessed with intelligence and leadership abilities should use their talents to help those who were less fortunate.

George Washington Carver

Remembering the Facts

1. He gained fame from his testimony before the House Ways and Means Committee on the hundreds of uses of the peanut.

2. He had a "green thumb;" his nickname was the "plant doctor."

3. He knew it would be hard for a black man to earn a living as an artist.

4. Tuskegee Institute

5. changing crop placement each year to enable the soil to rest and restore its nutrients

6. Any two of the following: fertilizing with manure; plowing under stalks and leaves of harvested plants; starting a compost heap

7. Any two of the following: traveled on weekends dispensing samples and advice; had monthly meetings at Tuskegee; wrote "Bulletins" containing practical advice; taught a free Short Course in Agriculture in the winter months

Understanding the Story

8. He thought his mission was to teach poor farmers to better themselves. He also enjoyed working in his own lab and in the fields.

9. They were all inventors. They all had innovative ideas for their time. They worked hard and stuck with their dreams.

10. Ecology tells us how we have depleted the earth's resources. We are looking to organic methods to restore the balance of nature and to eliminate toxic chemicals from our environment. We need to follow Carver's idea of conservation by using what we have on hand rather than depending on more technology.

Getting the Main Idea

He made outstanding advances in botany and shared his knowledge with small farmers. He rejuvenated agriculture in the South. He greatly improved the lot of poor farmers in the South.

Applying What You've Learned

Answers will vary.

Jackie Robinson

Remembering the Facts

1. Branch Rickey

2. His family lived in a lower middle class white neighborhood. Some of their white neighbors wanted them to leave and harassed them.

3. baseball, football, basketball

4. He was drafted at the beginning of World War II.

5. He convinced the army to allow blacks into OCS.

6. Most Valuable Player award

7. He was inducted into the Baseball Hall of Fame.

8. He traveled the country speaking for the NAACP. He worked with Dr. Martin Luther King Jr.

Understanding the Story

9. To win the respect of blacks and whites, Robinson needed to stand up for what was right without using physical force or threats. If he fought back, he would be sinking to the level of those who taunted him. He needed to win respect based on his ability to play the game.

10. He might have lost the respect of the players and fans. He wouldn't have been as popular.

11. If you are threatened, the first reaction is to fight back. That is the easy way. It is much harder to control yourself and ignore it.

Getting the Main Idea

Jackie Robinson opened pro baseball for African Americans. His courage and dignity won the respect of all.

Applying What You've Learned

by using prayer or meditation, focusing your thoughts, thinking of something else, etc.

Thurgood Marshall

Remembering the Facts

1. debating

2. They had to memorize sections of the U.S. Constitution.

3. Howard University

4. NAACP

5. *Brown* v. *the Board of Education*

6. It desegregated public schools.

7. U.S. Supreme Court Justice

8. Any two of the following: ending segregation and discrimination; getting rid of capital punishment; women's rights; constitutional rights of all Americans

Understanding the Story

9. Black schools did not have equal buildings, supplies, books, or teachers.

10. Laws can end discriminatory practices in the workplace, in schools, in housing, and in civil rights. With the law on their side, African Americans can make strides toward equality. However, laws cannot change people's attitudes. That takes time.

Getting the Main Idea

Thurgood Marshall used the law to fight discrimination and segregation. He championed the rights of all Americans.

Applying What You've Learned

Answers may include the following: fear of harassment; curiosity about the school and students; consciousness of differences and similarities

Rosa Parks

Remembering the Facts

1. Blacks were hired to do jobs that whites did not want to do. They were not allowed access to better jobs.

2. She had to drop out earlier to take care of her sick mother and grandmother.

3. get up and move to the back of the bus or get off the bus

4. Any two of the following: hire black drivers; be polite to blacks; have whites be seated from the front back and blacks from the back forward

5. They became violent. Police harassed black drivers. Ministers' homes were bombed. Shots were fired into homes and churches.

6. They were fired and could not get new jobs. They received constant threatening phone calls.

7. to provide education about black history

Understanding the Story

8. Rosa Parks got the ball rolling in the civil rights movement. Her simple act put many larger events in motion.

9. There were few schools for blacks and no transportation. Black children were often needed to work in the fields or at home to earn money.

10. It was a daily problem because most blacks rode the bus to work. It became an issue that was symbolic of all the segregation laws in the South.

Getting the Main Idea

Rosa Parks' simple act of courage triggered a series of much larger events, and led to the civil rights movement. From these events, blacks made great gains and had equal rights.

Applying What You've Learned

Students should mention her refusal to give up her seat on the bus, the books she has written, and the Rosa Parks Institute.

Dr. Martin Luther King Jr.

Remembering the Facts

1. They were laws that segregated blacks from whites. They existed mainly in the South.

2. the philosophy of passive resistance and nonviolence

3. The Supreme Court had just ruled to desegregate the schools. King knew things were about to happen and he wanted to be part of it.

4. the Southern Christian Leadership Conference (SCLC)

5. King wanted to be sure the Civil Rights Act passed.

6. He dreamed that one day people would live together peacefully. He hoped skin color would no longer be a factor.

7. the Nobel Peace Prize

Understanding the Story

8. On television the entire country could see what was happening in the South. Public opinion was influenced in favor of blacks and their desire for civil rights.

9. King would have been dismayed. He would have urged nonviolent protest instead.

10. Everyone respected him because of his ideas about nonviolence. After he was killed, he became a martyr for the cause.

Getting the Main Idea

King led the civil rights struggle with nonviolence, winning the sympathy and respect of the American people and winning great advances in black rights.

Applying What You've Learned

You would be unable to patronize many public places. You would be limited to substandard facilities reserved for blacks. You might be resigned to this treatment. You might be angry and resentful.

Malcolm X

Remembering the Facts

1. Omaha, Nebraska, in 1925

2. Any two of the following: three uncles were lynched; his house was set on fire by the Ku Klux Klan; his father was killed by the Klan

3. He converted to the Muslim religion. This inspired him to educate himself by reading all the books he could.

4. Any three of the following: no tobacco, alcohol, or drugs; black pride; black culture; family unity; education

5. Little was the name of the family that had owned Malcolm's ancestors long ago.

6. Dr. King advocated nonviolence while Malcolm X said African Americans should take their rights. King spoke of turning the other cheek while Malcolm X said to fight back if attacked. Dr. King favored integration while Malcolm X favored a separate black nation.

7. He saw Muslims of all colors living together in peace. He decided he should not hate all whites just because of the color of their skin. From then on, he judged people by their actions, not their skin color.

8. black pride; identity with black culture and heritage

Understanding the Story

9. He used words such as "revolution." He called for a separate black state. He told blacks they had waited long enough—they should take their rights by force. He told blacks to fight back if attacked.

10. His father was also a black militant who never quit speaking out about his beliefs, even when threatened with death.

Getting the Main Idea

Malcolm X gave many black males a sense of power and manhood. He fought for black freedom and justice. Many of his ideas are alive today, such as black pride, black cultural emphasis, and pride in black heritage.

Applying What You've Learned

You might like the idea of fighting back instead of turning the other cheek. He wants you to have rights now. His ideas of black culture and heritage could give you a sense of pride.

Jesse Jackson

Remembering the Facts

1. Jackson was the first serious black candidate for the Democratic nomination for president.

2. by his efforts to promote the civil rights movement

3. There were no segregation laws in Chicago. Most blacks were out of work and lived in the ghetto.

4. to encourage black-owned businesses and to get white-owned businesses to hire black workers

5. Jackson's multiethnic supporters were of all races and therefore of a "rainbow" of skin colors.

6. Any of the following: to protect civil rights; to work for equal opportunities in business and education; to bring peace to the world

7. He travels to countries around the world where he sees people being denied their rights. He also serves as a peace negotiator.

Understanding the Story

8. Poor African Americans did not have access to transportation, so they had to shop close to home. They did not have newspapers for comparison shopping, so they may not have realized they were paying too much.

9. African Americans could not easily open businesses because they could not get loans. Also, they faced much opposition from whites.

10. He believed in nonviolent resistance. King was Jackson's mentor and friend. Jackson used King's ideas of the boycott, the sit-in, and voter registration. Also, King inspired Jackson to enter the ministry. Both were religious men. Both were Southern Baptists.

Getting the Main Idea

Jesse Jackson has been the foremost black leader for many years. He has shown blacks that they can be leaders in the United States. He has been a strong voice for the poor and working class.

Applying What You've Learned

Answers include newspaper articles, TV coverage of the issue, letter-writing campaigns, picketing the business, boycotting the business, etc.

Maya Angelou

Remembering the Facts

1. "On the Pulse of Morning"

2. She taught her she could control her own future with hard work and courage. She encouraged her to read the works of black authors.

3. after she was raped as a child and did not speak for five years

4. Any three of the following: cook, cocktail waitress, streetcar conductor, dancer, singer, actress, writer

5. *I Know Why the Caged Bird Sings*

6. Robert Frost

7. You may have many defeats, but you must not be defeated. People are more alike than unlike.

Understanding the Story

8. She overcame many problems in her childhood and became a loving, optimistic, talented adult.

9. Clinton wanted to send the message that if we as a country face our problems with courage and hope and the belief that we can succeed, we'll be much more likely to succeed. This would set a positive tone for his new administration.

10. Americans are of many cultures and races. Yet we are all alike in that we are human. We have the same basic needs and the same hopes for our children.

Getting the Main Idea

Maya Angelou is an excellent poet and writer, but she is important because her writings embody the struggle of blacks for equal rights and acceptance. Her writings tell of the triumph of the human spirit over adversity.

Applying What You've Learned

Encourage students to make a list of the important ideals in their lives before they begin their poems.

Toni Morrison

Remembering the Facts

1. The Nobel Prize for Literature

2. Her father loved to spend time telling stories.

3. The books being studied were all ones she had already read. No black writers were included in the curriculum.

4. She saw how people lived in other areas of the country. She saw and experienced the racism in the South.

5. She was in a position to ensure that their books were published. She also gave them encouragement and a fair reading.

6. *Beloved* is the story of a woman who kills her child in order to prevent her from being a slave. The dead child comes back in the form of a young woman and tells her memories and the memories of all her black ancestors. The book seeks to portray the horrors of slavery.

7. *Jazz* and *Paradise*

Understanding the Story

8. Many people in American did not want to think about slavery and how horrible it really was. Toni wanted to be sure no one forgot that such horror had really happened in America. Her story was powerful and her language stunning. It was a masterpiece of writing.

9. Many people write to earn a paycheck. They are good at it and earn a good living. But others need to write even if they never earn any money from it. Toni felt a need to write and kept at it even when her books did not sell well.

10. Toni Morrison has loved to read all her life. She loves to write as well. So a reading room in a library is a perfect tribute.

Getting the Main Idea

Toni Morrison is the most influential black writer of her generation. As a writer she has the ability to make people think about important issues and perhaps to examine and change their attitudes.

Applying What You've Learned

The history of African Americans is entwined with the history of America. For years they were a silent, invisible part of America's history. Now their story is being told and has taken its rightful place as a part of America's story.

Additional Activities

Sojourner Truth

1. Make a time line of Sojourner Truth's life. Include illustrations of important events.

2. Create a word web to illustrate some of Sojourner Truth's outstanding personality traits.

3. Use the Internet to find out about laws that have been passed to give equal rights to women and blacks. Make a poster to display your findings. Some examples you might include are:

    • 13th amendment to the Constitution (outlawed slavery)

    • 15th amendment (gave blacks the right to vote)

    • Civil Rights Acts of 1964 and 1968 (forbade discrimination in hiring)

    • 19th Amendment (gave women the right to vote)

    • 24th Amendment (made it illegal to charge people to vote)

4. Read more about other women's rights leaders such as Susan B. Anthony, Elizabeth Cady Stanton, Harriet Tubman, Lucy Stone, Lucretia Mott, Julia Howe, Mary Wollstonecraft, Frances Willard, Emma Willard, Amelia Bloomer, Esther Morris, Francis Wright, Paulina Davis, and Harriet Beecher Stowe. Report on one of these women to the class.

5. Use the Internet to find out more about Quakers and their work for the antislavery movement in the mid-1800s.

Frederick Douglass

1. With a group, brainstorm a list of arguments you think Frederick Douglass might have used to convince others that slavery is wrong. Share your findings with the class.

2. Use the Internet to find information about the role black soldiers played in the Civil War.

3. Find out more about William Lloyd Garrison, an abolitionist who was young Douglass's hero.

4. Douglass and his wife, Anna, were involved in the Underground Railroad. Find out more about how they helped runaway slaves.

5. John Brown was a militant white abolitionist. He attacked the town of Harpers Ferry, Virginia. He hoped to hold the whites hostage and free the slaves. Read more about his story.

6. Read more about Frederick Douglass at http://www.pbs.org/wgbh/aia/part4/4p1539.html.

Harriet Tubman

1. Follow Harriet Tubman along the Underground Railroad at www.nationalgeographic.com/features/99/railroad.

2. Draw a picture illustrating something about the Underground Railroad.

3. Read about the life of Harriet Tubman and the Harriet Tubman Home at www.nyhistory.com/harriettubman/life.htm.

4. Harriet Tubman has been called "the black Moses." How do you think her story and the Bible story of Moses are similar?

5. Leading slaves to freedom was dangerous work. List some of the dangers faced by escaping slaves.

6. Write a poem or song about Harriet Tubman.

7. The Quakers are a religious group who were opposed to slavery. Read about the role of the Quakers in the Underground Railroad.

9. In 1831, when Harriet Tubman was about eleven years old, Nat Turner, a slave on a Virginia plantation, led an army of rebel slaves against their white masters. Other revolts were led by Gabriel Prosser in 1800 and Denmark Vesey in 1821. These revolts gave blacks hope and whites terror. Read more about one of these revolts and report on it to the class.

10. In 1619, the first slaves were brought to America, to Jamestown, Virginia. Read more about the slave trade between 1619 and 1808, and when it was made illegal to import slaves from Africa.

11. In 1793, Eli Whitney invented the cotton gin. This made raising cotton very profitable. More and more slaves were needed to work the cotton fields. Read more about Eli Whitney and the cotton gin.

12. Read Harriet Beecher Stowe's book *Uncle Tom's Cabin*, which tells of the life of a slave. Once, friends of Tubman invited her to see a play of *Uncle Tom's Cabin*. She refused, saying, "I've seen the real thing and I don't want to see it on any stage. Mrs. Stowe's pen hasn't begun to paint what slavery is."

Ida B. Wells-Barnett

1. Produce a newspaper front page that could have been written by Ida Wells-Barnett. Include news items, ads, and illustrations.

2. In the early 1900s many people died from yellow fever. The cause of the disease and its cure were not known. Find out more about yellow fever. Make a poster to illustrate your findings.

3. After the Civil War, southern whites used the threat of lynching to control blacks. Lynching is usually thought of as hanging. But at that time it meant any death by mob action without a trial. It was often hanging, but victims were also shot or burned. In small groups, discuss why you think whites were so violent toward blacks. Report your findings to the class.

Mary McLeod Bethune

1. Read the entire text of Bethune's "My Last Will and Testament." It can be found at www.nps.gov/archive/mamc/bethune/meet/will.htm. This work has been called one of the great historical documents of our time. Write a paragraph telling why you think it is so important.

2. Mary McLeod Bethune founded Bethune-Cookman College in Daytona Beach, Florida. Use the Internet to find more information about this school as it exists today: www.bethune.cookman.edu.

3. Bethune founded the National Council of Negro Women in 1935. Use the Internet to learn the achievements of this group. The web site is www.ncnw.org.

4. Work in small groups to brainstorm a list of necessities for starting a new school. If you had no money, how might you obtain these? Report your findings to the class.

Booker T. Washington

1. Have students stage a mock debate between Booker T. Washington and W.E.B. DuBois. Sample topics: Which should come first, education or the vote? Should the illiterate have the right to vote? segregation; the story of separate fingers on the hand

2. Tuskegee Institute is now Tuskegee University. Use the Internet to learn about Tuskegee and the work it does today. (www.tuskegee.edu) How does the school's curriculum today compare with that of the year it was founded? Are trades still emphasized? How many liberal arts courses are offered?

3. In 1900, Booker T. Washington started the National Negro Business League. Read and report on this group, which helped many black businesses get started.

4. Booker T. Washington wrote the story of his life in *Up from Slavery*. Read this book and report on it.

5. Frederick Douglass was America's black spokesperson for half a century. After Douglass's death in 1895, Booker T. Washington became the new leader. Make a Venn diagram to compare the ideas of the two men.

6. The cabin in which Booker T. Washington was born is now a national monument. See the cabin at www.nps.gov/bowa.

7. One of Washington's biographers said of him, "Washington accepted a half a loaf, not as a permanent settlement, but as a means toward obtaining the whole loaf later." Write a paragraph explaining what you think this means. Read your paragraph to the class.

W.E.B. DuBois

1. *The Souls of Black Folk: Essays and Sketches* was a best-seller when DuBois wrote it in 1903. Get a copy of this book and read one of the 14 essays it contains.

2. Use the Internet to research one of these topics: sharecropping, lynchings in the South, the Tuskegee Institute, the Niagara Movement, the NAACP, the Cotton Club, Harlem, *The Crisis*, Marcus Garvey, A. Philip Randolph, Paul Robeson, Langston Hughes,

Brown v. *Board of Education,* the Pan-African Conference, Jim Crow laws. Write a brief report and share your findings with the class.

3. DuBois wrote that education was the cure for the race problem. Do you agree or disagree? Write a paragraph explaining your answer.

4. DuBois learned about spirituals while he attended Fisk. The Fisk Jubilee Singers had made the world aware of these songs. Spirituals were a comfort to the slaves. They were also used to send secret messages among the slave community. Find out more about a spiritual. You may want to start with www.negrospirituals.com. Alone or in a group, sing or recite one of these spirituals for the class.

5. The 1920s have been called the "Renaissance" of African-American culture. In New York, things were happening at the Cotton Club in Harlem. Earl Hines, Count Basie and his orchestra, and Louis Armstrong were popular musicians. Poets and writers such as Claude McKay, Jean Toomer, Countee Cullen, and Langston Hughes enjoyed a large audience. Find out more about some of these artists.

6. DuBois was a national hero in Ghana because of his work in the Pan-African Movement. The President of Ghana, Kwame Nkrumah, invited DuBois to live in Ghana and work on an *Encyclopedia Africana.* When DuBois died, Ghana gave him a state funeral. In fact, DuBois is known as "the father of Africa." Find out more about his work in Africa.

7. During DuBois's lifetime (1868–1963) vast changes took place in America. In a small group, make a list as many of these as you can think of (for example: transportation, housing, lifestyle, education). Make a master list combining each group's findings on the board.

8. DuBois was the link between Frederick Douglass and Martin Luther King Jr. He knew both men. Write a paragraph telling how the three men were alike.

George Washington Carver

1. Make a poster illustrating the uses of the peanut.

2. Write a poem, song, or rap about George Washington Carver and the peanut.

3. George Washington Carver taught farmers how to make worn-out soil productive again. Read more about one of the following ideas: erosion by wind or water, soil depletion, crop rotation, organic farming, composting, or planting legumes to return nutrients to the soil. Make a poster to illustrate the procedure you chose.

4. By the mid-1800s, it was clear that farmers had used up much of the soil in America. The U.S. government gave money to the states to establish land-grant colleges for the study of agriculture. Find out about the land-grant college(s) in your state. Report on what this college does to benefit agriculture today.

5. Most black farmers in the South were sharecroppers. Read more about sharecropping and report your findings to the class.

6. Secretary of Agriculture James Wilson once told Carver, "You are probably doing more good to southern people than any other man in the South." In small groups, make a list of the ways Carver helped the southern people. Share your list with the class.

7. Use the Internet to learn more about George Washington Carver. Share your findings with the class.

Jackie Robinson

1. Make a word web using words that describe Jackie Robinson.

2. The second black player to join the Dodgers was Roy Campanella. Read more about his story.

3. It took Branch Rickey three years to find the right man to be the first black player in baseball. Make a list of the characteristics you think this black player would have to possess.

4. As a class, discuss this statement made by Robinson: "The richest treasure anybody has is his personal dignity."

5. Find out more about other blacks who played in the major leagues in the early days of integrated baseball. Some of these were Roy Campanella (1948), Don Newcombe (1949), and Willie Mays (1951).

6. Joe Louis was the first black heavyweight boxing champion of the world. Louis also faced an uphill struggle to make it to the top. Read more about his story.

Thurgood Marshall

1. Read more about Thurgood Marshall's life at www.thurgoodmarshall.com. Use the Internet to find out more about Charles Hamilton Houston, Marshall's mentor for many years.

2. Make a drawing that illustrates "separate but equal" schools and shows why they could never be "equal."

3. Read about Autherine Lucy and her fight to enroll at the University of Alabama, or James Meredith who became the first black to enroll at the University of Mississippi.

4. The 1896 case of *Plessy* v. *Ferguson* gave legal approval to the practice of segregation. Use the Internet to find out more about this case.

5. On July 1, 1991, President Bush nominated Clarence Thomas to the Supreme Court. Thomas became the second black to sit on the Supreme Court. Find out more about Clarence Thomas. Discuss how his ideas are different from Marshall's.

6. Marshall believed that justice could be achieved without violence and without black separatism. What would Martin Luther King Jr. or Malcolm X think about this view?

7. In 1980, a statue of Marshall was dedicated in Baltimore. Marshall said, "Some feel we have arrived. Others feel there is nothing more to do. I just want to be sure that when you see this statue, you won't think that's the end of it. I won't have it that way. There's too much work to be done." What do you think is the greatest "work" yet to be done by African Americans today?

Rosa Parks

1. Use the Internet to read about the Pathways to Freedom program. Find out what stops are included in the bus tour. (www.rosaparks.org)

2. *Time* magazine named Rosa Parks one of the most influential people of the twentieth century. In a small group, make a list of the five most influential people in America during the past year. On the board, make a master list as a class.

3. Just months before Rosa Parks refused to give up her seat on the bus, she attended Highlander Folk School in Tennessee. Read about Highlander. Explain what effect attending this school might have had on Parks.

4. Explain the term *boycott*. Use the Internet to find other examples of successful boycotts in history. Compile a list of the class's findings.

Dr. Martin Luther King Jr.

1. Construct a time line showing the important events of King's life. Illustrate your timeline.

2. As a class, discuss this topic: How do we as a society define an unjust law? What is the most effective way to change an unjust law?

3. Work in small groups to choose a rule in your school that students feel is unfair. Brainstorm possible effective ways to get this rule changed or modified. Report your results to the class.

4. Read a copy of "Letter from a Birmingham Jail" at http://almaz.com/nobel/peace/MLK-jail.html. Write a paragraph summarizing his main points.

5. Read the entire text of King's "I Have a Dream" speech. You can find this on the Internet at www.usconstitution.net/dream.html. Write a summary of his main points.

6. Mrs. Coretta Scott King began the Center for Nonviolent Change in Atlanta. Find out more about this center at www.thekingcenter.org.

7. Black and white students formed a group under the SCLC called the Student Nonviolent Coordinating Committee (SNCC). This group held sit-ins and peaceful protests all over the country. Read more about this group at www.ibiblio.org/sncc. Make a poster to illustrate your findings.

8. In the summer of 1961, black and white students rode buses together between cities in the South. They were called "Freedom Riders." Find out more about them and present your findings to the class.

9. The song of the civil rights protests was "We Shall Overcome." Learn this song. Teach the song to the class, and lead them in singing it.

10. Read more about James Earl Ray, King's assassin, and the two-month manhunt to capture him.

11. On King's tombstone are these words from his "I Have a Dream" speech: "Free at last! Free at last! Thank God Almighty I'm free at last." Write a paragraph in which you explain why you think these words were chosen for his tombstone?

12. In the summer of 1965, there were race riots in Watts, a black ghetto in Los Angeles. Read more about the Watts riots.

13. The Voting Rights Act became law in 1965, guaranteeing everyone the right to vote. Dr. King worked hard to get this law passed. Read more about the history of the Voting Rights Act.

Malcolm X

1. After Malcolm X's death, his wife, Betty Shabazz, worked for black rights. Read about her work.

2. Find out more about Malcolm X at www.brothermalcolm.net.

3. Malcolm X was killed in 1965. Discuss how history might have been different if he were still alive.

4. Malcolm X's father was a follower of Marcus Garvey, a black militant who advocated the return of African Americans to Africa to form a black nation called Liberia. Draw a map of Africa and label Liberia.

5. The leader of the Black Muslims was Elijah Muhammad. Find out more about Elijah Muhammad. Find out more about the teachings of the Black Muslims (also known as the Nation of Islam). Make a poster to illustrate the main teachings of this group.

6. After Malcolm X's death, his ideas were perpetuated by the Black Panther Party, which was led by Huey Newton and Bobby Seale. They called for the United States to be divided into two nations, one black and one white. Use the Internet to find out more about the Black Panthers.

7. Louis Farrakhan is another Black Muslim. Find out more about him on the Internet.

8. A famous convert to the Black Muslim religion was a boxer named Cassius Clay. Upon his conversion, he changed his name to Muhammad Ali. Ali has been a strong voice in the black community. Read more about him.

Jesse Jackson

1. Construct a time line showing the important events in Jesse Jackson's life.

2. Access the web site www.rainbowpush.org. Find out what issues the RainbowPUSH coalition is working on today. Make a poster showing their main projects.

3. In 1963, Jesse Jackson went to Selma, Alabama. He helped Dr. Martin Luther King form a march from Selma to Montgomery. Read more about the story of this famous march.

4. Make a Venn diagram to compare Jackson's philosophy to that of Malcolm X.

5. Jesse Jackson suffers from sickle-cell anemia. Find out more about this disease, which affects many African Americans. A good web site is www.scinfo.org.

6. Jesse Jackson was an outspoken opponent of apartheid in South Africa. Find out more about apartheid, which was finally abolished in 1993. Go to the web site http://www.africanaencyclopedia.com/apartheid/apartheid.html.

Maya Angelou

1. Learn more about Maya Angelou at her official web site: www.mayaangelou.com.

2. Read Angelou's first autobiography *I Know Why the Caged Bird Sings*. This outstanding book was nominated for the National Book Award in 1974.

3. Choose one of Angelou's poems. Memorize it and recite it for the class. Some of her books of poetry are:

    Just Give Me a Cool Drink of Water 'fore I Die (1971)

    Oh Pray My Wings Are Gonna Fit Me Well (1975)

    Shaker Why Don't You Sing (1978)

    And Still I Rise (1978)

    Shall Not Be Moved (1990)

4. Draw a picture to illustrate one of Angelou's poems.

5. Angelou's autobiography is made up of six volumes. Read one of these works:

    I Know Why the Caged Bird Sings (1970)

    Gather Together in My Name (1974)

    Singin' and Swingin' and Gettin' Merry Like Christmas (1976)

    The Heart of a Woman (1981)

    All God's Children Need Traveling Shoes (1986)

    A Song Flung Up to Heaven (2002)

6. Read the entire inaugural poem called "On the Pulse of Morning." Write a paragraph summarizing Angelou's message for all Americans.

7. Try writing some poetry yourself.

Toni Morrison

1. Read one of Morrison's novels and report on it to the class.

2. Get one of Morrison's short children's books she wrote with her son. Read it and report on it to the class.

3. Report to the class on another black author.

4. Read an online biography of Toni Morrison at http://us.penguingroup.com/nf/Author/AuthorPage/0,,1000023203,00.html?sym=BIO.

References

General References

Cohen, David and Collins, Charles M. *The African-Americans.* New York: Viking Penguin Books, 1993.

McKissack, Patricia and Fredrick. *The Civil Rights Movement in America.* Chicago: Children's Press, 1987.

Palmer, Colin A., Editor-in-Chief. *Encyclopedia of African-American Culture and History: The Black Experience in the Americas, 2nd edition.* Farmington Hills, MI: Thomson Gale, 2006.

Reynolds, Barbara. *And Still We Rise.* Washington, DC: Gannett Co., Inc., 1988.

Salley, Columbus. *The Black 100.* New York: Carol Publishing Group, 1993.

Smead, Howard. *The Afro-Americans.* New York: Chelsea House Publishers, 1989.

Smith, Jessie Carney, ed. *Epic Lives: 100 Black Women.* Detroit: Visible Ink Press, 1993.

——— . *Notable Black American Women.* Detroit: Gale Research, 1992.

Who's Who Among Black Americans, 1990/1991. 6th ed. Detroit: Gale Research, 1990.

Sojourner Truth

Ferris, Jeri. *Walking the Road to Freedom.* Minneapolis: Carolrhoda Books, Inc., 1988.

Krass, Peter. *Sojourner Truth: Antislavery Activist.* Philadelphia: Chelsea House Publishers, 2005.

McKissack, Patricia and Fredrick. *Sojourner Truth: A Voice for Freedom.* Hillside, NJ: Enslow Press, 1992.

Palmer, Colin A., Editor-in-Chief. *Encyclopedia of African-American Culture and History: The Black Experience in the Americas, 2nd edition.* Farmington Hills, MI: Thomson Gale, 2006.

Tolan, Mary. *Sojourner Truth.* Milwaukee: Gareth Stevens Children's Books, 1991.

Frederick Douglass

Douglass, Frederick. *Life and Times of Frederick Douglass.* New York: Collier Books, 1962.

——— . *Narrative of the Life of Frederick Douglass: An American Slave.* Cambridge: Belknap Press of Harvard University, 1960.

McKissack, Patricia and Fredrick. *Frederick Douglass: Leader Against Slavery.* Hillside, NJ: Enslow Publishers, 1991.

Palmer, Colin A., Editor-in-Chief. *Encyclopedia of African-American Culture and History: The Black Experience in the Americas, 2nd edition.* Farmington Hills, MI: Thomson Gale, 2006.

Russell, Sharman Apt. *Frederick Douglass: Abolitionist Editor*. Philadelphia: Chelsea House Publishers, 2005.

Harriet Tubman

Billingslea, Kathie. *Harriet Tubman*. New York: Ottenheimer Publishers, 1988.

Bradford, Sarah. *Harriet Tubman: The Moses of Her People*. Minneapolis: Carolrhoda Books, 1988.

Larson, Kate C. *Bound for the Promised Land: Harriet Tubman. Portrait of an American Hero*. New York: Ballantine Books, 2003.

Taylor, M. W. *Harriet Tubman*. New York: Chelsea House Publishers, 1991.

Weidt, Maryann N. *Harriet Tubman*. Minneapolis: Lerner, 2003.

Ida B. Wells-Barnett

McKissack, Patricia and Fredrick. *Ida B. Wells-Barnett: A Voice Against Violence*. Hillside, NJ: Enslow Publishers, 1991.

Palmer, Colin A., Editor-in-Chief. *Encyclopedia of African-American Culture and History: The Black Experience in the Americas, 2nd edition*. Farmington Hills, MI: Thomson Gale, 2006.

Steenwyk, Elizabeth. *Ida B. Wells-Barnett: Woman of Courage*. New York: Franklin Watts, 1992.

Thompson, Mildred I. *Ida B. Wells-Barnett: An Exploratory Study of an American Black Woman, 1893–1930*. Brooklyn, NY: Carlson Publishing, Inc., 1990.

Mary McLeod Bethune

Bethune, Mary McLeod. "My Last Will and Testament." *Ebony,* November 1992, pp. 108–112. (reprinted from August 1955 issue)

Greenfield, Eloise. *Mary McLeod Bethune*. New York: Thomas Y. Crowell Company, 1977.

Halasa, Malu. *Mary McLeod Bethune*. New York: Chelsea House Publishers, 1989.

Kelso, Richard. *Building a Dream*. Austin, TX: Steck-Vaughn, 1993.

Palmer, Colin A., Editor-in-Chief. *Encyclopedia of African-American Culture and History: The Black Experience in the Americas, 2nd edition*. Farmington Hills, MI: Thomson Gale, 2006.

Booker T. Washington

Frost, Helen. *Let's Meet Booker T. Washington*. Philadelphia: Chelsea Club House, 2004.

McKissack, Patricia and Fredrick. *Booker T. Washington*. New York: Chelsea House Publishers, 1992.

Palmer, Colin A., Editor-in-Chief. *Encyclopedia of African-American Culture and History: The Black Experience in the Americas, 2ⁿᵈ edition.* Farmington Hills, MI: Thomson Gale, 2006.

Schroeder, Alan. *Booker T. Washington.* New York: Chelsea House Publishers, 1992.

Washington, Booker T. *Up from Slavery.* (1901 original printing) New York: Viking Penguin, 1986.

W.E.B. DuBois

DuBois, W.E.B. *The Autobiography of W.E.B. DuBois: A Soliloquy on Viewing My Life from the Last Decade of Its First Century.* 1968.

McKissack, Patricia and Fredrick. *W.E.B. DuBois.* New York: Franklin Watts, 1990.

Palmer, Colin A., Editor-in-Chief. *Encyclopedia of African-American Culture and History: The Black Experience in the Americas, 2ⁿᵈ edition.* Farmington Hills, MI: Thomson Gale, 2006.

Stafford, Mark. *W.E.B. DuBois, Scholar and Activist.* Philadelphia: Chelsea House Publishers, 2005.

George Washington Carver

Adair, Gene. *George Washington Carver, Botanist.* New York: Chelsea House Publishers, 1989.

McMurray, Linda O. *George Washington Carver: Scientist and Symbol.* New York: Oxford University Press, 1981.

Palmer, Colin A., Editor-in-Chief. *Encyclopedia of African-American Culture and History: The Black Experience in the Americas, 2ⁿᵈ edition.* Farmington Hills, MI: Thomson Gale, 2006.

Rogers, Theresa. *George Washington Carver, Nature's Trailblazer.* Maryland: Twenty-first Century Books (Henry Holt & Co.), 1992.

Jackie Robinson

Diamond, Arthur. *The Importance of Jackie Robinson.* San Diego, CA: Lucent Books, 1992.

Frommer, Harvey. *Jackie Robinson.* New York: Franklin Watts, 1984.

Robinson, Jackie. *I Never Had It Made.* New York: G. P. Putnam's Sons, 1972.

Robinson, Sharon. *Promises to Keep: How Jackie Robinson Changed America.* New York: Scholastic Press, 2004.

Scott, Richard. *Jackie Robinson.* New York: Chelsea House Publishers, 1987.

Thurgood Marshall

Aldred, Lisa. *Thurgood Marshall: Supreme Court Justice.* Philadelphia: Chelsea House Publishers, 2005.

"The Legacy of Thurgood Marshall." *Ebony,* March 1993, pp. 126–130.

"Thurgood Marshall." *Current Biography,* September 1989, pp. 25–28.

Rosa Parks

Hull, Mary. *Rosa Parks: Civil Rights Leader.* Philadelphia: Chelsea House Publishers, 2005.

"Rosa Parks, 92, Founding Symbol of Civil Rights Movement, Dies." *The New York Times,* October 25, 2005. www.nytimes.com/2005/10/25/national/25parks.html.

"Rosa Parks." http://en.wikipedia.org/wiki/Rosa_Parks.

Dr. Martin Luther King Jr.

Davidson, Margaret. *I Have a Dream: The Story of Martin Luther King.* New York: Scholastic, Inc., 1985.

King, Martin Luther. "I Have a Dream" speech. Delivered August 28, 1963.

———. "Letter from a Birmingham Jail." Written 1963.

Patrick, Diane. *Martin Luther King Jr.* New York: Franklin Watts, 1990.

Palmer, Colin A., Editor-in-Chief. *Encyclopedia of African-American Culture and History: The Black Experience in the Americas, 2nd edition.* Farmington Hills, MI: Thomson Gale, 2006.

Smith, Kathie Billingslea. *Martin Luther King Jr.* New York: Julian Messner, 1987.

Malcolm X

"Malcolm X" H.N. Wilson Company, *Current Biography,* 1997.

"Malcolm X." *Encyclopedia of African-American Culture and History, 2nd edition. 2005.*

Malcolm X, with Alex Haley. *Autobiography of Malcolm X.* New York: Ballantine, 1965.

Palmer, Colin A., Editor-in-Chief. *Encyclopedia of African-American Culture and History: The Black Experience in the Americas, 2nd edition.* Farmington Hills, MI: Thomson Gale, 2006.

Rummel, Jack. *Malcolm X: Militant Black Leader.* Philadelphia: Chelsea House Press, 2005.

Jesse Jackson

"Jesse Jackson." *Contemporary Black Biography, Vol. 27.* Ed. by Ashyia Henderson. Gale Group, 2001.

"Jesse Jackson." *Current Biography Yearbook,* 1986, pp. 243–247.

"Jesse Jackson." http://en.wikipedia.org/wiki/Jesse_Jackson.

Otfinoski, Steven. *Jesse Jackson: A Voice for Change.* New York: Fawcett Columbine, 1989.

"RainbowPUSH Coalition." http://www.rainbowpush.org/about/history.html.

Maya Angelou

Angelou, Maya. *I Know Why the Caged Bird Sings.* New York: Random House, 1970.

———. "On the Pulse of Morning." 1993.

Haynes, Karima. "Prime-time Poet." Ebony, April 1993, pp. 68–72.

Official web site: www.mayaangelou.com.

Toni Morrison

Bloom, Harold, editor. *Toni Morrison's Beloved.* Chelsea House Publishers, 2004.

Century, Douglas. *Toni Morrison.* New York: Chelsea House Publishers, 1994.

Morrison, Toni. *Lecture and Speech of Acceptance, Upon the Award of the Nobel Prize for Literature.* New York: Alfred A. Knopf, 1994.

Sanna, Ellyn. "Biography of Toni Morrison." *Bloom's BioCritiques: Toni Morrison,* Harold Bloom, editor. Philadelphia: Chelsea House Publishers, 2002.

"Toni Morrison." http://en.wikipedia.org/wiki/Toni_Morrison

Share Your Bright Ideas

We want to hear from you!

Your name_____Date_____

School name_____

School address_____

City _____State _____Zip_____Phone number (_____)_____

Grade level(s) taught_____Subject area(s) taught_____

Where did you purchase this publication?_____

In what month do you purchase a majority of your supplements?_____

What moneys were used to purchase this product?

____School supplemental budget   ____Federal/state funding   ____Personal

Please "grade" this Walch publication in the following areas:

Quality of service you received when purchasing .... A   B   C   D

Ease of use... A   B   C   D

Quality of content.. A   B   C   D

Page layout .... A   B   C   D

Organization of material .... A   B   C   D

Suitability for grade level .... A   B   C   D

Instructional value.. A   B   C   D

COMMENTS:_____

_____

What specific supplemental materials would help you meet your current—or future—instructional needs?

_____

Have you used other Walch publications? If so, which ones?_____

May we use your comments in upcoming communications?   ___Yes   ___No

Please **FAX** this completed form to **888-991-5755**, or mail it to

Customer Service, Walch Publishing, P. O. Box 658, Portland, ME 04104-0658

We will send you a **FREE GIFT** in appreciation of your feedback. **THANK YOU!**